BY THE EDITORS OF CONSUMER GUIDE®

Mexican

COOKING CLASS COOKBOOK

BEEKMAN HOUSE
New York

Contents

Copyright © 1984 by Publications International, Ltd. All rights reserved. This book may not be reproduced or quoted in whole or in part by mimeograph or any other printed means or for presentation on radio, television, videotape, or film without written permission from:

Louis Weber, President
Publications International, Ltd.
3841 West Oakton Street
Skokie, Illinois 60076

Permission is never granted for commercial purposes.

On the Front Cover: (center) Crisp Beef & Chorizo Burritos and Fresh Tomato Salsa; (bottom) Chicken in Oaxacan Black Mole, with Refried Beans and Skillet Red Rice. *On the Back Cover:* Caramel Custard (Flan), Crisp Beef & Chorizo Burritos and Crumble-Top Orange Rolls.

Library of Congress Catalog Card Number: 84-61072
ISBN: 0-517-43544-6

This edition published by:
Beekman House
Distributed by Crown Publishers, Inc.
One Park Avenue
New York, New York 10016

Recipe Writing & Developing: Cynthia Scheer
Photography: Jim Johnson Photography
Food Styling for Photography: Yvonne Sutton

Manufactured in the United States of America
10 9 8 7 6 5 4 3 2 1

Introduction

Tacos, burritos, enchiladas—once foreign sounding, now they are practically as familiar as such earlier imports as pizza, quiche and egg rolls. It's no wonder that these Mexican dishes have been so readily accepted; who can resist the vibrant flavors, enticing texture contrasts and eye-catching colors of these fresh wholesome foods?

But Mexican cuisine is far more varied than the casual burrito-fancier might suspect. Based on such foods as corn, tomatoes, chilies and beans, this ancient cuisine developed over centuries, shaped by unique geography, climate, indigenous foods and the native Indian culture. It was enhanced—but not overshadowed—by the Spanish influence which began in the sixteenth century.

Mexican foods are sometimes mistakenly perceived as being heavy, oily and hot. However, the recipes in this book will certainly correct that misconception. Chosen to illustrate the wide variety this wonderful cuisine offers, they range from subtle to spicy, simple to complex, and rustic to sophisticated. Using authentic ingredients and cooking techniques, and presented with clear instructions and hundreds of how-to photos, the recipes are sure to please both novice and experienced cooks.

MEXICAN MEAL STYLES

The typical Mexican daily meal pattern differs from our own. It begins with *desayuno*, the first or small breakfast of coffee and sweet roll, eaten very early in the day. This is followed later in the morning by *almuerzo*, the second or heartier breakfast, usually including fruit, an egg dish, tortillas and beans.

The main meal, *comida*, is eaten in early to late afternoon. It consists of many courses, including appetizer, soup, a rice or noodle dish called *sopa seca* (dry soup), fish course, main course, salad, beans and dessert. This meal is generally (and understandably!) followed by a siesta.

After having a typical *comida*, all that is needed in the evening is a light snack, *merienda*, such as crusty rolls and sliced ham or a sweet roll and coffee. For special occasions, as on family birthdays or when entertaining guests, *cena*—a two- or three-course evening supper—is served.

The recipes in this book provide ample selection for those who wish to serve any of these typical Mexican meals. The recipes lend themselves equally well to including even just one or two into our more familiar meal pattern.

EQUIPMENT

Mexican cuisine requires very little in the way of specialized equipment, but a few items call for some discussion.

Bean Masher. A solid wooden block or perforated metal disk attached to a handle, this tool is very useful for the proper stirring and mashing needed to make Refried Beans. If necessary, a potato masher can be substituted.

Blender, Electric. Called a *liquidora* in Mexico, this is probably the most indispensable piece of equipment in the Mexican kitchen. It is used for grinding onion, garlic, fresh chilies and other ingredients before cooking and also for pureeing sauces before or after cooking. The blender is faster than a mortar and pestle for these tasks, and it allows more control and gives better results than does the food processor.

Comal. This is a round disk made of earthenware or metal, on which tortillas are cooked and garlic, spices, seeds and chilies are toasted. A cast-iron griddle or heavy, flat skillet can be used with good results.

Molcajete and Tejolote. These ancient implements of Mexi-can cooking have remained basically unchanged through the centuries. They are actually a mortar and pestle, composed of heavy, porous, brittle volcanic stone. The molcajete is shaped like a thick shallow bowl on three legs; the tejolote is a short, stubby, pointed piece of rock. Together, they are quite efficient in grinding whole spices and nuts to a powder and in grinding salsa or guacamole ingredients to the proper consistency. Although useful and interesting, they are not essential to any but the most serious cook. Depending on the specific function being performed, a regular mortar and pestle, spice grinder or blender can be used with satisfactory results.

Spice or Coffee Grinder, Electric. This small appliance is very effective in quickly grinding whole spices and preparing pure fresh chili powder from whole dried chilies. It is also used to grind seeds and nuts into the fine powder needed for some sauces, a function neither the blender nor food processor performs as well.

Tortilla Press. The press consists of 2 flat metal disks (usually 6 inches or 15 cm in diameter), hinged on one side, with a pressing handle attached at the opposite side. It is inexpensive and readily available in cookware shops and Mexican markets. A tortilla press is essential for speed and accuracy if you plan to make corn tortillas on a regular basis. However, you can improvise pressing with the bottom of a heavy skillet or pie plate.

MEXICAN INGREDIENTS

These ingredients are normally available in Mexican groceries. Many can be found in supermarkets and gourmet food stores; and some can be purchased in other Latin American, Caribbean and even Oriental food stores.

Annatto seeds (also called achiote): small, hard, crimson-colored seeds, used primarily in the Mayan-based cooking of the Yucatan. The seeds impart a deep yellow color and mild but distinctive flavor. They are soaked to soften or ground to a fine powder before using.

Chayote: a pear-shaped, pale green, soft-skinned squash with a delicious delicate flavor. It is sometimes called mirliton or christophine in non-Mexican markets.

Chilies: see the descriptions in the next section.

Chorizo: an orange- or red-colored, coarse-textured pork sausage sold bulk-style or stuffed into casings. The flavor ranges from highly seasoned to quite hot.

Coriander, fresh (also called cilantro or Chinese parsley): a pungent herb with green delicate leaves, similar in appearance, but not flavor, to flat-leaf parsley. Used extensively in Mexican cooking, there is no substitute. The dried leaf form is not acceptable and coriander seeds, although used in some Mexican dishes, are not interchangable with fresh coriander.

Corn husks, dried: used as wrappers for tamales, they must be soaked several hours before using. Look for packages in which the husks appear to have been cleaned well and do not have an excess of corn silk present.

Epazote: a pungent aromatic herb, available in stores in dried form. Fresh epazote can be grown from seed and can be found growing wild as lamb quarters.

Jícama: a root vegetable with thin tan-brown skin and crisp, sweetish, white flesh. It is shaped like a large turnip. Jícama is most often used raw in salads or eaten as a refreshing snack. It can also be found in Oriental markets.

Lard: the preferred cooking fat in Mexico, it imparts a rich, distinctive flavor which cannot be duplicated with other fats. For best flavor, fresh lard—available in Mexican markets or from a good butcher—is preferred. Highly purified and stabilized commercial lard is a weak but acceptable second choice. If necessary, substitute solid vegetable shortening for use in doughs and substitute vegetable oil for other cooking. For frying, a mixture of lard and shortening or oil can be used.

Masa harina: specially prepared flour used to make corn tortillas, tamales and other corn-based doughs. It is commonly available in 5-pound (2250-g) bags.

Mexican chocolate: a mixture of chocolate, almonds, sugar and sometimes cinnamon and vanilla, ground together and formed into round or octagonal tablets. It is used in desserts, to make a frothy chocolate beverage and, in small amounts, to add a subtle flavor enrichment to some mole sauces.

Mexican cream (crema) (see recipe on page 24): homemade cultured cream with a fresh, slightly sour taste and smooth, creamy consistency, similar to French crème fraîche. When used as a topping or accompaniment, commercial sour cream can be substituted, although sour cream is thicker and more tart. When used in sauces and other cooked mixtures, whipping cream can be substituted (as, in these cases, sour cream would curdle).

Onions: white onions with a sharp bite are used in Mexican cooking and are necessary for flavor balance and authenticity. (Yellow onions are too mild and impart an undesirable sweetness when cooked.)

Piloncillo: unrefined Mexican sugar formed into hard cone-shapes, available in many sizes. To measure piloncillo before using, grate it by hand on a vegetable shredder or place it in a sturdy plastic bag and pound it with a flat mallet into fine granules. Dark brown sugar can be substituted.

Queso añejo: an aged cheese, ranging from firm to very hard in texture, it has a fairly strong, salty flavor. The color ranges from creamy to pale yellow with an orange outer coating of paprika. Acceptable substitutes include grated Parmesan or Romano, crumbled feta or natural Gruyère.

Queso Chihuahua: a semi-soft cheese with creamy color, it is a rich cheese with mild flavor and good melting qualities. Mild Cheddar, Monterey Jack or Muenster are suitable substitutes.

Queso fresco: a fresh country- or ranch-style cheese, it is moist with a coarse, crumbly texture. White in color, queso fresco has a mild, slightly sour flavor. A dry cottage cheese or farmer's cheese with a little salt added can be substituted.

Tomatillo (also called tomate verde or Mexican tomato): a small, hard, green fruit with a papery outer husk which is pulled off before using. Tomatillos have a distinct acid flavor and are used extensively in cooked sauces. They are available fresh or canned (often labeled tomatillo entero). There is no substitute.

Tortillas: the mainstay of Mexican cuisine, these thin, flat breads are made of corn or wheat flour. Nothing can compare with the taste and texture of freshly made tortillas; but making them at home (see recipes on pages 26 and 30) requires some practice and skill. If desired, you can purchase tortillas as an acceptable substitute for use in any of the recipes in this book. They are readily available fresh, refrigerated or frozen. Corn tortillas usually measure between 5 and 6 inches (13 to 15 cm) in diameter; flour tortillas are available in many sizes, ranging from 7 to 12 inches (18 to 30 cm) in diameter.

CHILIES

The subject of chilies can be very confusing for those beginning to explore Mexican cuisine. There are perhaps over 100 varieties in Mexico, each with its own unique characteristics. They are used in fresh and dried form, whole and ground. The same chili can even be found under different names, depending upon its region of origin. Chilies range in hotness from very mild varieties to those which are incendiary; but hotness can vary even within a given variety, affected by such factors as regional climate and time of year in which the chili was grown.

Due to increasing interest in Mexican foods, chilies have become more readily available in this country. They can be found in Mexican groceries, in gourmet food stores and in many supermarkets. Not all chilies will be available in all areas at all times, however. For this reason, the following descriptions of the more common varieties are provided. With a basic knowledge of individual chili traits, you can usually manage very well with what is available. When preparing a particular dish, substitution of one chili for another is perfectly acceptable if the 2 chilies have similar traits. The character of the dish may change slightly, but will still be delicious and enjoyable.

A Note of Caution: The heat of the chili comes from a substance contained in the veins—the thin inner membranes to which the seeds are attached—and in the parts nearest the veins. For this reason, the veins and seeds are frequently removed and discarded. This substance can be very irritating to the skin and can cause painful burning of the eyes and lips. Do not touch your face while handling chilies and wash your hands well in warm soapy water after handling. Wear rubber gloves if your skin is especially sensitive.

Fresh Chilies

Fresh chilies will keep for several weeks refrigerated in a plastic bag lined with paper toweling. (The toweling will absorb moisture that may accumulate.) When purchasing fresh chilies, select those that have firm, unblemished skin.

Anaheim (also called California green chili): light green chili that has a mild flavor with a slight bite. It ranges from 4 to 6 inches (10 to 15 cm) in length, is about 1½ inches (4 cm) wide and has a rounded tip. Canned Anaheims are also available, whole or diced. For a spicier flavor, poblano chilies can be substituted.

Fresh chilies: (left to right) gueros, poblanos, jalapenos and serranos.

Dried chilies: (top, left to right) mulatos, anchos and guajillos; (bottom, left to right) pasillas, de arbols, pequins, japones and cascabels.

After toasting dried chilies, cut each open lengthwise; carefully pull out seeds and veins.

Güero: pale yellowish-green chili that is long and slender, usually ranging from 3 to 4 inches (8 to 10 cm) in length. Its flavor varies from mild to medium hot. Banana or cubanelle peppers can be substituted.

Jalapeño: small, dark green chili, normally 2 to 3 inches (5 to 8 cm) long and about ¾ inch (2 cm) wide, with a blunt or slightly tapered end. The flavor of jalapeños varies from hot to very hot. They are also available canned and pickled. Serranos, finger peppers or any small, hot, fresh chilies can be substituted.

Poblano: very dark green, large, triangular-shaped chili with a characteristic pointed end. Poblanos are usually 3½ to 5 inches (9 to 13 cm) long. Their flavor ranges from mild to quite hot. For a milder flavor, Anaheims can be substituted.

Serrano: medium green, very small chili, with very hot flavor. It usually ranges from 1 to 1½ inches (2.5 to 4 cm) in length and is about ⅜ inch (1 cm) wide with a pointed end. Serranos are also available pickled. Jalapeños, finger peppers or any small, hot, fresh chilies can be substituted.

Dried Chilies

Dried red (ripe) chilies are usually sold in cellophane packages of various sizes and weights. They will keep indefinitely if stored in a tightly covered container in a cool, dark, dry place.

Ancho: fairly large, triangular-shaped chili, only slightly smaller than the mulato chili. It has wrinkled, medium to dark reddish-brown skin. Anchos are full-flavored, ranging from mild to medium-hot.

Cascabel: small, round chili with fairly smooth, dark red skin. Its flavor ranges from medium-hot to hot.

Chipotle: this is the jalapeño chili which has been smoked and dried. It has wrinkled, medium-brown skin and a rich, smoky, very hot flavor. Chipotles are also commonly available canned in adobo sauce.

De árbol: quite small, slender, almost needle-shaped chili with smooth, bright red skin and very hot flavor.

Guajillo: medium-size chili with a long, narrow shape and fairly smooth, dark red skin. Its flavor is quite hot. (Guajillos are sometimes labeled as "cascabels.")

Japonés: orangish to bright red chili, with smooth to slightly wrinkled skin. This small chili (slightly larger than the de árbol) has a long, slender shape and a very hot flavor.

Mulato: triangular-shaped, large chili that has wrinkled, blackish-brown skin. Its flavor is rich, pungent and medium-hot.

Pasilla: long, slender, medium-size chili with wrinkled, blackish-colored skin. It has a pungent flavor, ranging from mild to quite hot. (Pasillas are sometimes labeled "negro chilies.")

Pequín: very tiny chilies, shaped like oval beads. They have slightly wrinkled, orangish-red skins. Use pequín chilies with caution as their flavor is very, very hot. (These are sometimes labeled "tepin chilies.")

Pure, fresh chili powder: any of the above dried chilies, seeded and ground into fine powder. Commercial chili powders are usually blends of chili powder with other ingredients, such as cumin and oregano; they are normally available in only one level of hotness and can become stale in a fairly short period of time. With pure, fresh chili powder, you can choose from mild to medium-hot to very hot and will get a truer, fresher chili flavor. Grind your own pure chili powders with an electric spice grinder or purchase them in small packets in Mexican groceries and some gourmet food stores.

HELPFUL PREPARATION TECHNIQUES

Roast, peel, seed and devein fresh chilies. Using tongs to hold chili, place each chili directly in medium flame of gas burner; roast, turning as needed, until chili is evenly blistered and charred. Place roasted chili into plastic bag immediately; close the plastic bag. Repeat with remaining chilies. (Or place chilies on foil-lined broiler rack; roast, turning as needed, 2 to 3 inches or 5 to 8 cm from broiler heat source until evenly blistered and charred.)

Let roasted chilies stand in closed plastic bag 20 minutes. Peel each chili under cold, running water, rubbing and pulling off charred skin. Slit chili open lengthwise using scissors or knife. Carefully pull out and discard seeds and veins. Rinse well and drain; pat dry with paper toweling.

Broil tomatoes. Place whole tomatoes on foil-lined broiler rack; place 4 inches (10 cm) from broiler heat source. Broil, turning as needed, until tomatoes are evenly blistered and dark brown (not black) on outside and soft throughout, 15 to 20 minutes. Use entire tomato; do not skin, seed or core.

Toast garlic. Heat ungreased comal, griddle or heavy skillet over medium heat. Cook unpeeled garlic on comal, pressing down with spatula and turning over occasionally, until dark brown outside and soft throughout, 1 to 3 minutes.

Toast, seed and devein dried chilies. Heat ungreased comal, griddle or heavy skillet over medium heat; place chilies on comal in a single layer. Cook chilies, pressing down with spatula and turning over occasionally, until color changes slightly (but do not burn) and chilies become fragrant (but not to the point of emitting a harsh aroma), 1 to 3 minutes. If toasting a large number of dried chilies, they can be placed in a single layer in 350°F (180°C) oven until the chilies are hot to the touch and fragrant, 3 to 5 minutes. When chilies are cool enough to handle but still pliable, cut each open lengthwise with scissors; carefully pull out seeds and veins. Rinse and rub chilies under cold running water only if specified in the recipe.

Soften and warm tortillas. Heat ungreased comal, griddle or heavy skillet over medium heat. Sprinkle both sides of each tortilla lightly with a few drops of water; place tortilla on comal and heat, turning once, just until soft and warm, 15 to 20 seconds per side. Stack tortillas and enclose in aluminum foil until all have been softened and warmed. Or, you can use a microwave oven for this procedure. Stack tortillas and wrap in plastic wrap; microwave on high power, turning over and rotating ¼ turn once, about 1 minute.

After roasting and bagging fresh chilies, peel charred skin under cold, running water (left). Slit chili open lengthwise (center). Carefully pull out and discard seeds and veins (right).

Chalupas & Gorditas

1 cup (250 mL) Refried *Black* Beans (see Index), cheese omitted
Chilied Meat Filling (recipe follows)
½ to ¾ cup (125 to 180 mL) Fresh Tomato Salsa (see Index)
2 cups (500 mL) masa harina
3 tablespoons (45 mL) lard or vegetable shortening, melted
3 tablespoons (45 mL) grated queso añejo
2 small fresh jalapeño chilies, seeded, minced
Pinch salt
1¼ cups (310 mL) warm chicken stock or broth
Lard or vegetable oil
Crumbled queso añejo
Radish slices
Ripe olive slices
Fresh coriander leaves and sprigs

1. Prepare Refried Black Beans, omitting cheese.

2. Prepare Chilied Meat Filling.

3. Prepare Fresh Tomato Salsa.

4. Mix masa harina, 3 tablespoons (45 mL) each melted lard and grated cheese, the chilies and salt in medium

bowl. Add stock; stir to form soft dough which holds together when pressed with hand. If dough is dry and crumbly, add extra stock, 1 teaspoon (5 mL) at a time; if wet and sticky, add extra masa harina, 1 teaspoon (5 mL) at a time.

5. Divide dough into 24 even pieces. For gorditas, shape 12 pieces into balls; flatten into ¼-inch (6-mm) thick rounds. For chalupas, shape 12 pieces into 2-inch (5-cm) long bars; flatten into ¼-inch (6-mm)

thick ovals. Pinch up edges of rounds and ovals to make ½-inch (1.3-cm) high lips. Pinch ends of ovals to make boat shapes.

6. Melt enough lard in deep, heavy, large skillet for ¼-inch (6-mm) depth. Heat over medium-high heat until very hot, but not smoking. Fry 5 or 6 dough shells at a time: add shells to skillet, flat-side-down; fry 1 minute. Spoon hot lard into center of each shell; fry 1 minute longer. Turn shells over; fry until golden, about 1 minute longer. Remove with slotted spatula; drain on paper toweling. Keep warm in 250°F (120°C) oven until all have been fried.

7. Quickly reheat beans and meat filling. Spread 2 teaspoons (10 mL) beans in bottom of each shell; add 1 tea-

spoon (5 mL) salsa or to taste. Top with about 1 tablespoon (15 mL) meat filling. Garnish with crumbled cheese, radish and olive slices and coriander. Serve immediately.

Makes 24 appetizers

Chilied Meat Filling

2 tablespoons (30 mL) lard or vegetable oil
1 pound (450 g) boneless pork shoulder or beef chuck, cut into ½-inch (1.3-cm) cubes
1½ cups (375 mL) water
6 dried cascabel or 2 dried ancho chilies
1 cup (250 mL) boiling water
1 tablespoon (15 mL) chopped white onion
2 cloves garlic
Pinch salt

1. Melt lard in large saucepan over medium-high heat. Add meat; cook, stirring occasionally, until brown on all sides, about 5 minutes. Remove and discard all fat.

2. Add 1½ cups (375 mL) water to pan. Heat to simmering; reduce heat to low. Simmer, partially covered, until meat is tender, 20 to 30 minutes. Cool completely.

3. Meanwhile, seed and devein chilies; place in small bowl. Add boiling water; let stand 30 minutes.

4. Drain chilies well. Combine chilies, onion, garlic and salt in blender container; process until smooth. If needed, add cooking liquid from meat, 1 tablespoon (15 mL) at a time, to make smooth puree.

5. Drain meat; return to pan. Add chili puree. Cook and stir over medium heat until sauce is thickened and coats meat heavily, about 10 minutes.
Makes about 2 cups (500 mL)

Seafood-Filled Avocados AGUACATES CON MARISCOS

1 tablespoon (15 mL) fresh
    lime juice
1 tablespoon (15 mL) cider
    vinegar
1 clove garlic, minced
½ teaspoon (2 mL) grated
    lime rind
¼ teaspoon (1 mL) salt
⅛ to ¼ teaspoon (0.5 to
    1 mL) crumbled, seeded,
    dried de árbol or japonés
    chili
¼ cup (60 mL) vegetable oil
4 ounces (115 g) cooked crab
    meat
8 ounces (225 g) tiny shelled,
    deveined, cooked shrimp
2 tablespoons (30 mL)
    coarsely chopped fresh
    coriander
2 large firm-ripe avocados
2 cups (500 mL) shredded
    Romaine lettuce
Red bell-pepper strips
4 green olives
4 lime wedges

1. Combine lime juice, vinegar, garlic, lime rind, salt and chilies in small bowl. Gradually add oil, whisking continuously; whisk dressing until thoroughly blended.

2. Break crab meat into coarse shreds, picking out and discarding any shell or cartilage.

3. Combine crab, shrimp and coriander in medium bowl. Add dressing; toss lightly with

2 forks to mix. Refrigerate, covered, to blend flavors, 1 to 2 hours.

4. At serving time, cut avocados lengthwise into halves. Remove and discard pits; pare halves.

5. Divide lettuce evenly among 4 individual serving plates. Top each with 1 avocado half, cut-side-up. Spoon ¼ of the seafood mixture into hollow of each avocado. Garnish with bell-pepper strips and olives. Serve with lime wedges.

Makes 4 servings

Melted Cheese with Chorizo QUESO FUNDIDO CON CHORIZO

Onion Relish Veracruz
    (recipe follows)*
24 (4-inch or 10-cm) corn
    tortillas OR 6 (8-inch or
    20-cm) flour tortillas, cut
    into quarters
8 ounces (225 g) queso
    Chihuahua or Monterey
    Jack cheese
4 to 6 ounces (115 to 170 g)
    chorizo

Fresh Tomato Salsa (see Index) or Green Salsa (see Index) may be used in place of Relish.

1. Prepare Onion Relish Veracruz.

2. Heat oven to 400°F (200°C). Wrap tortillas in aluminum foil.

3. Cut cheese into very thin slices. Arrange slices in even layer in 4 to 6 ovenproof plates or shallow casseroles (about 5-inch or 13-cm diameter and less than 1 inch or 2.5 cm deep) or in 1 large, shallow casserole (about 12-inch or 30-cm diameter).

4. Remove and discard casing from chorizo. Heat medium skillet over high heat; reduce heat to medium. Crumble chorizo into skillet; cook, stirring frequently and breaking up into small pieces, until

brown, 6 to 8 minutes. Remove with slotted spoon; drain on paper toweling. Keep warm.

5. Place cheese in oven; bake 3 minutes. Add tortillas to oven; bake until cheese is melted and bubbly and tortillas are hot, about 4 minutes longer.

6. Place tortillas in serving bowl; sprinkle chorizo evenly over cheese. Serve immediately: Spoon cheese mixture onto tortilla and top with Onion Relish; fold tortilla around filling.

Makes 4 to 6 servings

Onion Relish Veracruz

1 medium white onion
1 or 2 fresh jalapeño chilies
3 tablespoons (45 mL) fresh
    lime juice
½ teaspoon (2 mL) salt

1. Cut onion lengthwise in half. Cut halves lengthwise into very thin slices; separate into slivers.

2. Cut chilies lengthwise into halves; remove and discard seeds. Cut halves lengthwise into very thin slivers.

3. Combine all ingredients in small bowl; mix well. Let stand, covered, at room temperature to blend flavors, 2 to 3 hours.

Makes about 1 cup (250 mL)

Cheese Turnovers with Green Salsa QUESADILLAS Y SALSA VERDE

Green Salsa (recipe follows)
8 ounces (225 g) queso Chihuahua or Muenster cheese
1½ cups (375 mL) masa harina
½ cup (125 mL) all-purpose flour
1 teaspoon (5 mL) baking powder
¾ to 1 cup (180 to 250 mL) warm water
Vegetable oil

1. Prepare Green Salsa.

2. Cut cheese into 1×¼×¼-inch (2.5×0.6×0.6-cm) pieces.

3. Mix masa harina, flour and baking powder in medium bowl. Add ¾ cup (180 mL) warm water; stir until thoroughly blended. Stir in as much of the remaining water as needed, 1 tablespoon (15 mL) at a time, just until dough holds together.

4. Divide dough into thirds; shape each into ball. Flatten balls into 1-inch (2.5-cm) thick

rounds; cut each into 8 even wedges. Roll each wedge of dough into ball between palms; flatten slightly. Place 6-inch (15-cm) square of waxed paper on lower plate of tortilla press. Place ball slightly off center (away from handle) on paper; top with second square

of waxed paper. Press down firmly with top of tortilla press to make 3½-inch (9-cm) tortilla.

5. Carefully peel waxed paper from both sides of tortilla. Place 4 to 6 pieces of cheese on

one half of tortilla; fold other half over cheese. Pinch edges together to seal. Cover turnovers with kitchen towel to prevent drying.

6. Heat oven to 250°F (120°C). Pour oil into deep, heavy, large skillet to depth of 1 inch (2.5 cm). Heat oil to 375°F (190°C); adjust heat to maintain temperature.

7. Fry 3 or 4 turnovers at a time, turning once, until crisp and light brown, 1½ to 2 minutes. Remove with slotted spoon; drain on paper toweling. Keep warm in oven on paper-towel-lined baking sheet until all have been fried. Serve immediately with Green Salsa.

Makes 24 turnovers

Green Salsa

½ cup (125 mL) lightly packed fresh coriander leaves
1 can (4 ounces or 115 g) diced green chilies
3 or 4 fresh jalapeño chilies, seeded
3 tablespoons (45 mL) fresh lime juice
1 clove garlic, minced
½ teaspoon (2 mL) salt

1. Combine all ingredients in blender or food processor container. Process until almost smooth. Let stand, covered, at room temperature to blend flavors, 1 to 2 hours.

Makes about ¾ cup (180 mL)

Nachos

1½ cups (375 mL) Refried Beans (see Index), cheese omitted
6 dozen Corn Tortilla Chips (see Index)
1½ cups (375 mL) shredded Monterey Jack cheese
1½ cups (375 mL) shredded mild Cheddar cheese
1 large tomato, seeded, chopped
½ cup (125 mL) thinly sliced pickled jalapeño chilies

1. Prepare Refried Beans, omitting cheese.

2. Prepare Corn Tortilla Chips.

3. Heat oven to 400°F (200°C). Mix Jack and Cheddar cheeses in small bowl. Reheat Refried Beans, if necessary.

4. Spread 1 teaspoon (5 mL) beans on each tortilla chip.

5. Arrange chips in single layer, with edges slightly overlapping, on 2 or 3 baking sheets or large ovenproof platters.

6. Sprinkle chips evenly with tomato and chilies; top with cheese mixture.

7. Bake until cheese is melted and bubbly, 5 to 8 minutes. Serve immediately.

Makes 6 dozen nachos

Corn Tortilla Chips TOSTADITAS

12 (6-inch or 15-cm) corn
tortillas, preferably
day-old
Lard or vegetable oil
½ to 1 teaspoon (2 to 5 mL)
salt

1. If tortillas are fresh, let
stand, uncovered, in single
layer on wire rack 1 to 2 hours
to dry slightly.

2. Stack 6 tortillas; cutting
through stack, cut tortillas into
6 or 8 equal wedges. Repeat
with remaining tortillas.

3. Melt enough lard in deep,
heavy, large skillet for ½-inch
(1.3-cm) depth. Heat to 375°F
(190°C); adjust heat to maintain
temperature.

4. Add as many tortilla wedges
to skillet as will fit in single
layer. Fry, turning occasionally,
until crisp, about 1 minute.
Remove with slotted spoon;
drain on paper toweling. Repeat until all chips have been
fried. Sprinkle chips with salt.
Makes 6 or 8 dozen chips

Chili Variation: When all chips
have been fried, pour off lard
remaining in skillet. Sprinkle
chips evenly with salt and 1 to 2
teaspoons (5 to 10 mL) pure,
hot chili powder. Return chips
to skillet; cook over low heat,
stirring constantly but lightly,
until chili powder is fragrant,
45 seconds to 1 minute. (Do not
let chili powder burn.) Transfer
chips to basket or bowl; let cool
slightly.

Note: *Tortilla chips are served
with salsas as a snack, used as the
base for nachos and used as scoops
for guacamole, other dips or refried
beans. They are best eaten fresh,
but can be stored, tightly covered,
in cool place 2 or 3 days. Reheat in
350°F (180°C) oven a few minutes
before serving.*

Guacamole

4 tablespoons (60 mL) finely
chopped white onion
1½ tablespoons (22 mL)
coarsely chopped fresh
coriander
1 or 2 fresh serrano or
jalapeño chilies, seeded,
finely chopped
¼ teaspoon (1 mL) chopped
garlic, if desired
2 large soft-ripe avocados
1 medium very ripe tomato
Boiling water
1 to 2 teaspoons (5 to 10 mL)
fresh lime juice
½ teaspoon (2 mL) salt
Corn Tortilla Chips (recipe
above)

1. Combine 2 tablespoons
(30 mL) onion, 1 tablespoon
(15 mL) coriander, the chilies
and garlic in molcajete (or large
mortar). Grind with tejolote (or
pestle) until almost smooth.
(Mixture can be processed
in blender, if necessary; but it will
become more watery than desired.)

2. Cut avocados lengthwise
into halves; remove and discard pits. Scoop avocado flesh
out of shells; add to chili mixture. Mash roughly, leaving
avocado slightly chunky.

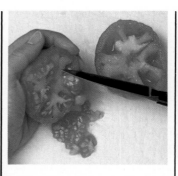

3. Place tomato in small saucepan of boiling water to loosen
skin, 30 to 45 seconds. Rinse
immediately under cold running water. Peel tomato; cut
crosswise in half. Gently
squeeze each half to remove
and discard seeds. Chop tomato.

4. Add tomato, lime juice, salt
and remaining 2 tablespoons
(30 mL) onion and ½ tablespoon (7 mL) coriander to avocado mixture; stir to mix well.
Transfer to serving bowl. Guacamole is best served immediately, but can be refrigerated,
covered, up to 4 hours. Serve
with Corn Tortilla Chips.
Makes about 2 cups (500 mL)

Mexican Pizzas TOSTADAS DE HARINA

Red & Green Salsa (recipe
 follows)
8 ounces (225 g) chorizo
1 cup (250 mL) shredded
 mild Cheddar cheese
1 cup (250 mL) shredded
 Monterey Jack cheese
3 (10-inch or 25-cm) flour
 tortillas

1. Prepare Red & Green Salsa.

2. Remove and discard casing
from chorizo. Heat medium
skillet over high heat; reduce
heat to medium. Crumble

chorizo into skillet; cook, stirring frequently and breaking
up into small pieces, until
brown, 6 to 8 minutes. Remove
with slotted spoon; drain on
paper toweling.

3. Heat oven to 450°F (230°C).
Mix Cheddar and Jack cheeses
in small bowl.

4. Place tortillas on baking
sheets. Top with chorizo, dividing evenly, leaving ½ inch
(1.3 cm) of tortilla edges uncovered. Sprinkle cheese mixture over chorizo.

5. Bake, uncovered, until
edges are crisp and golden and
cheese is bubbly, 8 to 10 minutes.

6. Transfer to serving plates;
cut each pizza into 6 wedges.
Serve immediately. Sprinkle
Red & Green Salsa on pizzas,
as desired.

Makes 6 to 8 servings

Red & Green Salsa

1 small red bell pepper
¼ cup (60 mL) coarsely
 chopped fresh coriander
3 green onions, thinly sliced
2 fresh jalapeño chilies,
 seeded, minced
2 tablespoons (30 mL) fresh
 lime juice
1 clove garlic, minced
¼ teaspoon (1 mL) salt

1. Cut bell pepper lengthwise
in half; remove and discard
seeds and veins. Cut halves
lengthwise into thin slivers; cut
slivers crosswise into halves.

2. Combine all ingredients in
small bowl; mix well. Let
stand, covered, at room temperature to blend flavors, 1 to 2
hours.

Makes about 1 cup (250 mL)

Piquant Marinated Fish SEVICHE DE PESCADO

1 pound (450 g) whitefish,
 pompano or mackerel
 fillets, skinned
3 to 4 limes
1 medium tomato, peeled,
 seeded, diced
1 to 3 fresh jalapeño chilies,
 seeded, finely chopped*
2 tablespoons (30 mL) olive
 or vegetable oil
1 tablespoon (15 mL) drained
 capers
½ teaspoon (2 mL) salt
¼ teaspoon (1 mL) dried
 oregano
½ firm-ripe avocado
½ red onion
4 to 6 lime wedges

*The crunch of fresh chilies is
needed for this dish; do not substitute canned. If fresh jalapeños
are not available, use serranos or
any fresh, hot chilies.*

1. Cut fish fillets into ½-inch
(1.3-cm) square pieces.

2. Squeeze limes to yield ¾
cup (180 mL) juice.

3. Combine fish and lime juice
in medium glass bowl (not
metal or plastic); mix well. Refrigerate, covered, stirring
gently occasionally, until fish
becomes firm and opaque, at
least 4 hours. (The acid of the
lime juice "cooks" the fish.)

4. About 1½ hours before
serving, add tomato, chilies,
oil, capers, salt and oregano to
fish mixture; mix gently. Refrigerate, covered, until serving time.

5. At serving time, pare avocado; cut lengthwise into 4 to 6
slices. Cut onion into thin
slices.

6. Arrange onion slices around
edge of 4 to 6 large scallop
shells or individual serving
plates. Spoon fish mixture with
slotted spoon into center of
each shell. Garnish with avocado slices; serve with lime
wedges.

Makes 4 to 6 servings

Seafood Soup SOPA DE MARISCOS

1 pound (450 g) sea bass,
   black bass or red snapper
   fillets
1 pound (450 g) pompano,
   mackerel or swordfish
   fillets or steaks
1 pound (450 g) fresh
   medium shrimp, in shells
1½ dozen fresh clams or
   oysters, in shells
2 quarts (2 L) Rich Fish Broth
   (recipe follows)*
3 pounds (1350 g) tomatoes,
   broiled (see page 5)
3 tablespoons (45 mL) lard or
   vegetable oil
½ cup (125 mL) minced
   white onion
3 cloves garlic, minced
1 tablespoon (15 mL) tomato
   paste
2 tablespoons (30 mL) white
   vinegar
2 bay leaves
½ teaspoon (2 mL) dried
   oregano
½ teaspoon (2 mL) dried
   thyme
¼ teaspoon (1 mL) salt
⅛ teaspoon (0.5 mL) freshly
   ground black pepper
Lime wedges
Chopped fresh coriander
Chopped fresh jalapeño
   chilies

*Bottled clam broth can be sub-
stituted, if necessary.

1. Cut fish fillets and steaks
into 2-inch (5-cm) squares, discarding any bones. Shell and
devein shrimp, reserving
shells for Rich Fish Broth.

Scrub clams (or oysters) under
cold running water with wire
brush. Refrigerate all seafood,
covered.

2. Prepare Rich Fish Broth.

3. Process tomatoes in blender
until smooth. Heat lard in
6-quart (6-L) Dutch oven over
medium heat until hot. Add
onion and garlic; saute until
soft, about 3 minutes. Add

tomatoes and tomato paste;
cook, stirring constantly, 5
minutes.

4. Add Fish Broth, vinegar, bay
leaves, oregano, thyme, salt
and pepper to Dutch oven.
Heat to boiling; reduce heat to
medium-low. Simmer, cov-
ered, 20 minutes.

5. Add clams to soup; cook,
covered, over medium heat 2
minutes. Add fish and shrimp.
Simmer, covered, until fish is
opaque throughout and clams
have opened slightly, 5 to 6
minutes. Discard any un-
opened clams.

6. Ladle soup into individual
bowls. Serve immediately;
pass lime, coriander and chilies
to be added according to individual taste.

   Makes 4 main-course
   or 8 first-course servings

Rich Fish Broth

3 pounds (1350 g) bones,
   heads and trimmings from
   sea bass or other non-oily
   fish
Shells from 1 pound (450 g)
   shrimp
1 medium white onion, cut in
   half
1 dried de árbol chili, seeded
1 sprig fresh parsley
1 bay leaf
3 whole black peppercorns
2½ to 3 quarts (2.5 to 3 L)
   cold water

1. Combine all ingredients except water in 6-quart (6-L) ket-
tle. Add enough water to cover
solids by 2 inches (5 cm). Heat
over medium-high heat to boiling; reduce heat to low. Simmer, uncovered, 30 minutes.

2. Strain broth through sieve
or colander lined with several
thicknesses dampened cheese-
cloth; discard solids. Broth can
be refrigerated, covered, up to
2 days or frozen up to 2 weeks.
Makes about 2½ quarts (2.5 L)

Jaliscan Hominy Soup POZOLE

3 pounds (1350 g) country-
style spareribs
2 tablespoons (30 mL) lard or
vegetable oil
1 cup (250 mL) finely
chopped white onion
6 cloves garlic, thinly sliced
1½ teaspoons (7 mL) salt
1 teaspoon (5 mL) dried
oregano
½ teaspoon (2 mL) cumin
seeds, coarsely crushed
1½ quarts (1.5 L) water
3 pounds (1350 g) chicken
backs, wings and necks
1 pig's foot (cracked), if
desired*
Fresh Tomato Salsa (see
Index)
1 can (29 ounces or 825 g)
hominy, rinsed, drained
Shredded iceberg lettuce
Sliced radishes
Sliced green onions
Lime wedges

*The pig's foot adds body to soup; it
can be omitted, or a few pork neck
bones can be substituted, if desired.*

1. Trim fat from spareribs. Cook ribs, ½ at a time, in lard in 6- to 7-quart (6- to 7-L) Dutch oven over medium heat, turning occasionally, until brown on all sides, 30 to 40 minutes. Remove ribs from pan.

2. Add white onion to pan; saute over medium heat until soft, about 4 minutes. Add garlic, salt, oregano and cumin; saute 30 seconds.

3. Add water, chicken, pig's foot and spareribs to pan. Heat over medium heat to boiling; reduce heat to very low. Simmer, covered, skimming foam occasionally, until ribs are tender, 2 to 2½ hours.

4. Remove and discard chicken and pig's foot. Remove spareribs to plate; let stand until cool enough to handle, about 20 minutes. Remove and discard fat and bones from ribs. Break

meat into large chunks; return to soup. Refrigerate, covered, 4 hours or overnight.

5. Prepare Fresh Tomato Salsa.

6. Remove and discard fat from top of soup. Stir in hominy. Heat over medium heat to boiling; reduce heat to low. Simmer, covered, 30 minutes. Ladle soup into individual bowls. Pass lettuce, radishes, green onions, lime wedges and Fresh Tomato Salsa to be added according to individual taste.

**Makes 4 to 6 main-course
or 8 first-course servings**

Tortilla Soup SOPA DE TORTILLA

6 to 8 (6-inch or 15-cm) corn
tortillas, preferably
day-old
2 large very ripe tomatoes,
peeled, seeded
⅔ cup (160 mL) coarsely
chopped white onion
1 large clove garlic
Lard or vegetable oil
7 cups (1750 mL) chicken
stock or broth
4 sprigs fresh coriander
3 sprigs fresh mint, if
desired
½ to 1 teaspoon (2 to 5 mL)
salt
4 or 5 dried pasilla chilies
5 ounces (140 g) queso
Chihuahua or Monterey
Jack cheese, cut into
½-inch (1.3-cm) cubes
¼ cup (60 mL) coarsely
chopped fresh coriander

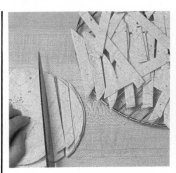

1. Stack tortillas; cut into ½-inch (1.3-cm) wide strips. Spread loosely on wire rack; let stand 1 or 2 hours to dry slightly.

2. Combine tomatoes, onion and garlic in blender container; process until smooth. Heat 3 tablespoons (45 mL) lard in 3-quart (3-L) saucepan over

medium heat until hot. Add tomato mixture; cook, stirring frequently, 10 minutes.

3. Add stock and coriander sprigs to pan; heat over high heat to boiling. Reduce heat to low; simmer 20 minutes. Add mint and salt; simmer 10 minutes longer. Remove and discard coriander and mint sprigs; keep soup hot, covered.

4. Melt enough lard in heavy, large skillet for ½-inch (1.3-cm) depth. Heat to 375°F (190°C); adjust heat to maintain temperature.

5. Fry ½ tortilla strips at a time in lard, turning occasionally, until crisp, about 1 minute. Remove with slotted spoon; drain on paper toweling.

6. Fry chilies in lard, turning occasionally, until puffed and crisp, about 30 seconds. Do not let chilies burn. Drain on paper toweling. Cool slightly. Crumble chilies coarsely.

7. Ladle soup into bowls; pass chilies, tortilla strips, cheese and chopped coriander to be added according to individual taste.

Makes 4 to 6 servings

Fresh Tomato Gazpacho

6 large very ripe tomatoes
(about 3 pounds or 1350 g)
1½ cups (375 mL) tomato
juice
1 small clove garlic
2 tablespoons (30 mL) fresh
lime juice
2 tablespoons (30 mL) olive
oil
1 tablespoon (15 mL) white
wine vinegar
1 to 1½ teaspoons (5 to
7 mL) salt
1 teaspoon (5 mL) sugar
½ teaspoon (2 mL) dried
oregano
6 green onions, thinly sliced
¼ cup (60 mL) finely
chopped celery
¼ cup (60 mL) finely
chopped, seeded, unpared
cucumber
1 or 2 fresh jalapeño chilies,
seeded, minced
Garlic Croutons (recipe
follows)
1 cup (250 mL) diced avocado
1 red or green bell pepper,
seeded, chopped
2 tablespoons (30 mL) fresh
coriander leaves

Lime wedges
Mexican Cream (see Index)
or sour cream, if desired

1. Seed and finely chop 1 to-mato; reserve.

2. Coarsely chop remaining 5 tomatoes. Combine ½ of these tomatoes, ¾ cup (180 mL) tomato juice and the garlic in blender container; process un-

til smooth. Press through sieve into large bowl; discard seeds. Repeat with remaining coarsely chopped tomatoes and ¾ cup (180 mL) tomato juice.

3. Whisk lime juice, oil, vin-egar, salt, sugar and oregano into tomato mixture. Stir in re-served finely chopped tomato, the green onions, celery, cu-cumber and chilies. Refrigerate soup, covered, at least 4 or up to 24 hours to blend flavors.

4. Prepare Garlic Croutons.

5. Stir soup well; ladle into chilled bowls. Pass Garlic Croutons, avocado, bell pep-per, coriander, lime and Mexi-can Cream to be added accord-ing to individual taste.

Makes 6 to 8 servings

Garlic Croutons

5 slices firm white bread
2 tablespoons (30 mL) olive
oil
1 small clove garlic, minced
¼ teaspoon (1 mL) paprika

1. Heat oven to 300°F (150°C). Trim and discard crusts from bread. Cut bread into ½-inch (1.3-cm) cubes.

2. Heat oil in medium skillet over medium heat until hot; stir in garlic and paprika. Add bread; cook and stir just until bread is evenly coated with oil, about 1 minute.

3. Spread bread on large bak-ing sheet. Bake until crisp and golden, 20 to 25 minutes. Cool completely.
Makes about 2 cups (500 mL)

Black Bean Soup SOPA DE FRIJOL NEGRO

8 ounces (225 g) dried black
beans (1¼ cups or
310 mL)
5 cups (1250 mL) cold water
2 bay leaves
3 tablespoons (45 mL) lard or
vegetable oil
½ cup (125 mL) chopped
white onion
1 clove garlic, minced
1 large tomato, peeled,
seeded, chopped
¾ to 1 teaspoon (4 to 5 mL)
salt
½ teaspoon (2 mL) dried
oregano
⅛ to ¼ teaspoon (0.5 to
1 mL) ground dried
pequín chili
Thinly sliced fresh jalapeño
chilies
Sliced green onions
Lime wedges

1. Rinse beans thoroughly in sieve under cold running water, picking out debris or blemished beans.

2. Combine beans, water and bay leaves in 3- to 4-quart (3- to 4-L) heavy saucepan. Heat over high heat to boiling; im-mediately reduce heat to very low. Simmer, covered, just un-til beans are tender but not soft, 1½ to 2 hours.

3. Heat lard in medium skillet over medium heat until hot. Add onion and garlic; saute until soft, about 4 minutes. Add tomato, salt, oregano and pequín chili; cook and stir over

medium-high heat until mix-ture is almost dry, about 5 min-utes.

4. Add tomato mixture to beans; simmer, covered, stir-ring occasionally, until beans are soft, about 30 minutes. Remove and discard bay leaves.

5. Press soup mixture a few times with bean masher or po-tato masher to very roughly mash beans.

6. Serve soup, garnished with jalapeño chilies and green on-ions, accompanied by lime wedges.
Makes 4 or 5 servings

Chicken Soup CALDO DE POLLO

4 medium carrots
1 large yellow summer squash or zucchini (about 10 ounces or 285 g)
6 cups (1.5 L) chicken stock or broth
2 unpeeled cloves garlic, toasted (see page 5)
¾ to 1 teaspoon (4 to 5 mL) salt
½ teaspoon (2 mL) dried oregano
Pinch ground cumin
2 whole chicken breasts (about 1 pound or 450 g each)
2 dried guajillo chilies, toasted (see page 5)
1 tablespoon (15 mL) coarsely chopped fresh coriander
Lime wedges

1. Cut carrots lengthwise into halves; cut halves crosswise into 3-inch (8-cm) lengths. Cut squash crosswise into ¼-inch (6-mm) thick slices.

2. Place carrots, stock, garlic, salt, oregano and cumin in 5-quart (5-L) Dutch oven; heat to boiling. Add chicken and chilies; reduce heat to low. Simmer, covered, just until chicken is tender, 15 to 20 minutes.

3. Remove chicken to plate; let stand until cool enough to handle, about 10 minutes.

4. Meanwhile, add squash to stock mixture. Simmer, covered, over low heat just until crisp-tender, 5 to 7 minutes.

Remove from heat. Remove and discard chilies and garlic, taking care not to let chilies break and release seeds.

5. Remove and discard skin and bones from chicken. Tear chicken into coarse shreds. Add chicken and coriander to soup. Cook over medium heat just until hot, 1 to 2 minutes. Serve with lime wedges.

Makes 4 to 6 servings

Corn Soup SOPA DE ELOTE

5 or 6 medium ears fresh corn, husked*
3½ cups (875 mL) chicken stock or broth
½ to ¾ teaspoon (2 to 4 mL) salt
2 fresh poblano chilies, roasted, peeled, seeded, deveined (see page 5)
3 tablespoons (45 mL) butter or margarine
1 large tomato, broiled (see page 5)
¼ cup (60 mL) coarsely chopped white onion
½ teaspoon (2 mL) dried oregano
½ cup (125 mL) whipping cream

*If unavailable, substitute 2 packages (10 ounces or 285 g each) frozen whole kernel corn; cook in Step 2 until tender, 4 to 5 minutes.

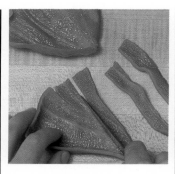

1. Cut corn kernels from cobs with knife; scrape cobs with spoon to remove pulp. You will need 4 cups (1 L) kernels and pulp.

2. Combine corn, stock and salt in 3-quart (3-L) saucepan. Heat to boiling; reduce heat to low. Simmer, covered, until corn is tender, 8 to 10 minutes.

3. Remove ½ cup (125 mL) corn from pan with slotted spoon; reserve. Process remaining corn and stock, ½ at a time, in blender until smooth. Return to saucepan.

4. Cut chilies lengthwise into ½-inch (1.3-cm) wide strips; cut strips crosswise into 2- or 3-inch (5- or 8-cm) lengths. Saute chilies in butter in medium skillet over medium heat until limp and tender, 4 to 5 minutes. Remove with slotted spoon; reserve.

5. Process tomato, onion and oregano in blender until smooth. Heat butter remaining in skillet over medium heat until hot; add tomato mixture. Cook and stir until thickened, 4 to 5 minutes.

6. Add tomato mixture to corn mixture in saucepan; heat to boiling. Reduce heat to low; simmer 5 minutes.

7. Remove soup from heat; gradually stir in cream. Cook over very low heat just until hot, about 30 seconds; do not boil. Serve soup immediately, garnished with reserved corn and chilies.

Makes 4 to 6 servings

Chicken Flautas FLAUTAS DE POLLO

3 chicken breast halves
(about 1½ pounds or
675 g)
1 can (4 ounces or 115 g)
diced green chilies
½ cup (125 mL) water
½ teaspoon (2 mL) salt
½ teaspoon (2 mL) ground
cumin
Fresh Tomato Salsa (recipe
follows)
1 cup (250 mL) Guacamole
(see Index)
16 (6-inch or 15-cm) corn
tortillas
Vegetable oil
4 cups (1 L) shredded iceberg
lettuce
1 cup (250 mL) shredded
Monterey Jack cheese
½ cup (125 mL) Mexican
Cream (recipe follows) or
sour cream
Tomato wedges
Fresh coriander sprigs

1. Combine chicken, chilies, water, salt and cumin in medium skillet. Heat over medium-high heat to boiling; reduce heat to low. Simmer, covered, until chicken is tender, 15 to 20 minutes. Remove chicken to plate; let stand until cool enough to handle. Drain chilies; reserve.

2. Prepare Fresh Tomato Salsa. Prepare Guacamole.

3. Remove and discard skin and bones from chicken; pull chicken into long thin shreds. If not freshly made, soften and warm tortillas (see page 5).

4. Heat oven to 250°F (120°C). Pour oil into deep, heavy skillet to depth of 1 inch (2.5 cm). Heat oil to 375°F (190°C); adjust heat to maintain temperature.

5. For each flauta: Overlap 2 tortillas by about ½. Spoon ⅛ of chicken lengthwise down center; top with ⅛ of chilies. Roll up as tightly as possible.

6. Fry 1 or 2 flautas at a time in oil, holding closed with tongs during first 30 seconds to prevent unrolling. Fry, turning occasionally, until crisp and golden on all sides, about 2 minutes. Drain on paper toweling. Keep warm in oven on paper-towel-lined baking sheet until all have been fried.

7. Divide lettuce evenly among 4 serving plates. Top each with 2 flautas. Top with ¼ each of cheese, Guacamole and Mexican Cream. Garnish with tomato and coriander. Serve immediately with Fresh Tomato Salsa.

Makes 4 servings

Fresh Tomato Salsa

1 medium tomato, finely
chopped
¼ cup (60 mL) coarsely
chopped fresh coriander
2 tablespoons (30 mL) finely
chopped white onion
1 fresh jalapeño chili,
seeded, finely chopped
1 tablespoon (15 mL) fresh
lime juice

1. Combine all ingredients in small bowl; stir to mix well. Let stand, covered, at room temperature to blend flavors, 1 to 2 hours.

Makes about ¾ cup (180 mL)

Mexican Cream

1 cup (250 mL) whipping
cream
2 tablespoons (30 mL)
cultured buttermilk

1. Heat cream in small saucepan over medium-low heat just until barely warm to the touch (90 to 100°F or 32 to 38°C); transfer to clean bowl or jar.

2. Stir buttermilk into cream. Let stand at warm room temperature, covered with plastic wrap, until cream begins to thicken, 8 to 16 hours.

3. Stir cream until smooth. Refrigerate, covered, at least 1 day to allow tart flavor to develop. Mexican Cream can be stored in refrigerator up to 2 weeks.

Makes about 1 cup (250 mL)

Creamy Chicken Enchiladas   ENCHILADAS SUIZAS

1 broiler-fryer chicken (about 3½ pounds or 1.6 kg), cut into 8 pieces
3 fresh poblano chilies, roasted, peeled, seeded, deveined (see page 5), diced
1 large tomato, peeled, seeded, chopped
½ cup (125 mL) finely chopped white onion
1 clove garlic, minced
¾ teaspoon (4 mL) salt
½ teaspoon (2 mL) ground cumin
½ cup (125 mL) chicken stock or broth
1½ cups (375 mL) whipping cream
12 (6-inch or 15-cm) corn tortillas
2 cups (500 mL) shredded queso Chihuahua or Monterey Jack cheese
Sliced green onion tops
Red bell pepper slivers

1. Arrange chicken pieces in single layer in 12-inch (30-cm) skillet. Sprinkle with chilies, tomato, onion, garlic, salt and cumin; add stock. Heat over medium-high heat to boiling; reduce heat to low. Simmer, covered, until chicken is very tender, about 1 hour.

2. Remove chicken pieces from skillet with tongs, shaking off pieces of vegetables. Let chicken stand until cool enough to handle.

3. Skim and discard fat from top of stock mixture in skillet. Heat mixture to boiling; boil gently over medium-high heat, stirring frequently, until reduced to 2 cups (500 mL), 6 to 8 minutes. Transfer mixture to 13×9×2-inch (33×23×5-cm) baking dish.

4. Remove and discard skin and bones from chicken. Tear chicken into coarse shreds.

5. Heat oven to 375°F (190°C). Heat cream in medium skillet over medium heat until just below boiling; remove from heat.

6. Dip 1 tortilla in hot cream until limp, a few seconds; remove, draining off excess

cream. Spread 1/12 of the chicken (about 3 tablespoons or 45 mL) down center of tortilla; roll up and place seam-side-down on sauce in baking dish. Repeat with remaining tortillas and chicken. Pour remaining cream evenly over enchiladas.

7. Sprinkle enchiladas evenly with cheese. Bake until sauce is bubbly and cheese is melted and golden, 25 to 30 minutes. Garnish with green onion and bell pepper.

Makes 4 to 6 servings

Corn Tortillas   TORTILLAS DE MAIZ

2 cups (500 mL) masa harina
1 to 1¼ cups (250 to 310 mL) warm water

1. Cut two 7-inch (18-cm) squares from heavy-duty plastic bag. Mix masa harina and 1 cup (250 mL) water in medium bowl. Add as much remaining water as needed, 1 tablespoon (15 mL) at a time, mixing with hand to form smooth stiff dough.

2. Test consistency of dough as follows: Roll 1 piece dough into 1¾-inch (4.5-cm) ball; flatten slightly. Place ball on piece of plastic on lower plate of tortilla press, slightly off-center away

from handle.* Cover with second piece of plastic; press down firmly with top of press to make 6-inch (15-cm) tortilla. Peel off top piece of plastic;

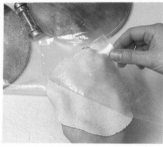

invert tortilla onto hand and peel off second piece of plastic. If edges are cracked or ragged, dough is too dry; mix in 1 or 2 teaspoons (5 to 10 mL) water at a time until dough presses out with smooth edges. If tortilla sticks to plastic, dough is too wet; mix in 1 tablespoon (15 mL) masa harina at a time until dough no longer sticks when pressed.

3. When dough has correct consistency, divide into 12 equal pieces for 6-inch (15-cm) tortillas or into 24 pieces for 4-inch (10-cm) tortillas. Shape pieces into balls; cover with plastic wrap to prevent drying.

4. Press out tortillas as in Step 2, stacking between sheets of plastic or waxed paper.

5. Heat ungreased heavy griddle or skillet over medium-high heat until a little water flicked on surface dances in tiny droplets. Carefully lay 1 tortilla on griddle; cook until edges begin to dry out, about 30 seconds. Turn tortilla over; cook second side until dry and lightly flecked with brown

spots, 45 seconds to 1 minute. Turn tortilla over again; cook first side until dry and light brown, 15 to 30 seconds longer. During last stage of cooking, tortilla may puff up; do not press it down. Remove tortilla to kitchen towel; it will be slightly stiff, but will soften as it stands.

6. Cook remaining tortillas as in Step 5. If griddle becomes too hot after cooking a few, reduce heat to prevent burning. Stack cooked tortillas and keep wrapped in towel until all are cooked. Use immediately or wrap in foil and keep warm in 250°F (120°C) oven up to 30 minutes. Tortillas are best when fresh, but can be wrapped in foil and refrigerated up to 3 days or frozen up to 2 weeks; reheat in 250°F (120°C) oven before using.

Makes 12 (6-inch or 15-cm) or 24 (4-inch or 10-cm) tortillas

A tortilla press works best, but if necessary, you can press with bottom of pie plate or heavy skillet.

Stacked Enchiladas ENCHILADAS CHATAS

Red Chili Sauce (see Index)
1 pound (450 g) ground beef
¾ cup (180 mL) plus 1
    tablespoon (15 mL)
    vegetable oil
1 cup (250 mL) finely
    chopped white onion
1 clove garlic, minced
½ teaspoon (2 mL) salt
12 (6-inch or 15-cm) corn
    tortillas
2 cups (500 mL) shredded
    mild Cheddar cheese
⅔ cup (160 mL) chopped,
    pitted ripe olives
1½ cups (375 mL) shredded
    iceberg lettuce

1. Prepare Red Chili Sauce.

2. Cook beef in 1 tablespoon (15 mL) oil in 10-inch (25-cm) skillet over medium-high heat, breaking up beef into small pieces, until no longer red, 6 to 8 minutes. Add onion; saute until onion is soft, about 4 minutes. Spoon off fat.

3. Add garlic, salt and 1 cup (250 mL) Red Chili Sauce to skillet; mix well. Heat over medium heat to boiling; reduce heat to low. Simmer, uncovered, stirring frequently, until most of the liquid has evaporated and meat is moistly coated with sauce, about 5 minutes.

4. Heat remaining ¾ cup (180 mL) oil in medium skillet over medium heat until hot. Fry tortillas, 1 at a time, just until limp and blistered, 5 to 10 seconds per side. Drain on paper toweling. Remove oil from skillet; wipe clean.

5. Heat remaining 1½ cups (375 mL) Chili Sauce in medium skillet over medium heat until hot; remove from heat.

6. Dip 1 tortilla into Chili Sauce to coat both sides; remove, draining off excess sauce. Place on broiler-proof individual serving plate. Spread tortilla with slightly rounded ¼ cup (60 mL) meat mixture; sprinkle with 2 tablespoons (30 mL) cheese and 1 tablespoon (15 mL) olives. Add second dipped tortilla and meat, cheese and olive layers; top

with third dipped tortilla. Repeat procedure to assemble 3 more stacks. Pour any remaining Chili Sauce over stacks and sprinkle with remaining cheese, dividing evenly.

7. Place stacks under broiler so that tops are 4 inches (10 cm) below heat source. Broil until cheese is melted, about 3 minutes. Sprinkle tops with remaining olives, dividing evenly. Garnish with lettuce.

Makes 4 servings

Pork & Tortilla Casserole CHILAQUILES DE PUERCO

8 (6-inch or 15-cm) corn
    tortillas, preferably
    day-old
2 pounds (900 g) boneless
    pork shoulder, cut into
    1½-inch (4-cm) cubes
2 medium white onions,
    thinly sliced lengthwise
1 teaspoon (5 mL) salt
Water
Lard or vegetable oil
2 fresh poblano chilies,
    roasted, peeled, seeded,
    deveined (see page 5),
    chopped
1 clove garlic, minced
½ teaspoon (2 mL) ground
    cumin
1 can (13 ounces or 370 g)
    tomatillos, undrained,
    coarsely chopped
1 cup (250 mL) whipping
    cream
¼ cup (60 mL) coarsely
    chopped fresh coriander
1 cup (250 mL) shredded
    queso Chihuahua or
    Monterey Jack cheese
1 cup (250 mL) shredded
    mild Cheddar cheese
5 or 6 tomato slices, cut into
    halves

½ cup (125 mL) Mexican
    Cream (see Index) or sour
    cream
Fresh coriander sprigs

1. Stack tortillas. Cut in half; then cut crosswise into ½-inch (1.3-cm) wide strips. Spread loosely on wire rack; let stand 1 to 2 hours to dry slightly.

2. Combine pork, 1 onion and salt in large saucepan; add water to cover pork. Heat over high heat to boiling; reduce heat to low. Simmer, covered, until pork is tender, 1½ hours.

3. Melt enough lard in deep, heavy, large skillet for ½-inch (1.3-cm) depth. Heat to 375°F (190°C); adjust heat to maintain

temperature. Fry tortilla strips in lard, about ⅓ at a time, stirring and turning occasionally, until crisp, about 1 minute. Remove with slotted spoon; drain on paper toweling.

4. Heat 2 tablespoons (30 mL) lard in 10-inch (25-cm) skillet over medium heat until hot. Add remaining onion; saute until soft, about 4 minutes. Add chilies, garlic and cumin;

saute 1 minute. Stir in undrained tomatillos. Heat to boiling; reduce heat to low. Simmer, covered, 15 minutes. Add whipping cream to skillet; cook, uncovered, over medium-high heat, stirring frequently, until mixture is re-

duced to 2⅔ cups (660 mL), 10 to 12 minutes. Stir in chopped coriander.

5. Heat oven to 375°F (190°C). Mix cheeses in small bowl. Drain pork; using 2 forks, pull into coarse shreds.

6. Spread ½ of tortilla strips in greased, shallow 2½-quart (2.5-L) casserole. Add layers of ½ each pork, cream mixture and cheeses in that order. Repeat all layers.

7. Bake until hot throughout and golden on top, 25 to 30 minutes. Garnish with tomato slices, Mexican Cream and coriander sprigs.

Makes 4 to 6 servings

Crisp Beef & Chorizo Burritos CHIMICHANGAS

Fresh Tomato Salsa (see Index)
6 ounces (170 g) chorizo
1 pound (450 g) ground beef
½ cup (125 mL) finely chopped white onion
1 clove garlic, minced
½ teaspoon (2 mL) ground cumin
1 can (8 ounces or 225 g) tomato sauce
¼ cup (60 mL) sliced, pitted ripe olives
12 (8-inch or 20-cm) flour tortillas
1 cup (250 mL) shredded Muenster or Monterey Jack cheese
Vegetable oil
1 cup (250 mL) Mexican Cream (see Index) or sour cream
Fresh coriander sprigs
Radishes

1. Prepare Fresh Tomato Salsa.

2. Remove and discard casing from chorizo. Heat 10-inch (25-cm) skillet over high heat about 45 seconds; reduce heat to medium. Crumble chorizo into skillet; cook, stirring frequently 5 minutes.

3. Crumble beef into skillet. Cook over medium-high heat, breaking meat up into small pieces, until no longer red, 6 to 8 minutes. Add onion, garlic and cumin; cook and stir until onion is soft, about 4 minutes. Spoon off and discard excess fat.

4. Add tomato sauce to skillet; mix well. Heat over high heat to boiling; reduce heat to low. Simmer, covered, 15 minutes. Uncover skillet; cook and stir over medium heat until most of

the liquid has evaporated and meat is moistly coated with sauce, about 5 minutes. Stir in olives.

5. If not freshly made, soften and warm tortillas (see page 5).

6. For each burrito, place about ¼ cup (60 mL) meat mixture

on bottom half of 1 tortilla; spread to within 1½ inches (4 cm) of bottom and side edges. Sprinkle with slightly rounded tablespoon (15 mL) cheese.

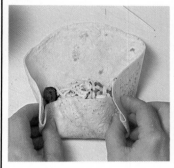

7. Fold bottom edge of tortilla up over filling; fold in right and left edges. Roll up to completely enclose filling; fasten top with wooden pick.

8. Heat oven to 250°F (120°C). Pour oil into deep, heavy skillet to depth of 1 inch (2.5 cm). Heat oil to 375°F (190°C); adjust heat to maintain temperature.

9. Fry 3 burritos at a time, turning once, until golden, 2 to 3 minutes. Remove with tongs; drain on paper toweling. Keep warm in oven on paper-towel-lined baking sheet until all have been fried.

10. To serve, remove wooden picks; place 2 burritos on each serving plate. Top with large dollop Mexican Cream and small spoonful of Fresh Tomato Salsa. Garnish with coriander and radishes; serve immediately with remaining salsa.
Makes 6 servings

Flour Tortillas TORTILLAS DE HARINA

2 cups (500 mL) all-purpose flour
½ teaspoon (2 mL) salt
¼ cup (60 mL) vegetable shortening
½ cup (125 mL) warm water

1. Mix flour and salt in medium bowl. Rub shortening into flour with fingertips until mixture has fine, even texture. Stir in water until dough forms.

2. Knead dough on floured surface until smooth and elastic, 2 to 3 minutes. Let rest, wrapped in plastic wrap, at room temperature, 30 minutes.

3. Knead dough a few times; divide into 8 even pieces for 10-inch (25-cm) tortillas or into 12 even pieces for 8-inch (20-cm) tortillas. Roll each piece into ball; cover with plastic wrap to prevent drying.

4. Using rolling pin, roll out each dough ball on floured surface, turning over frequently, into 8- or 10-inch (20- or 25-cm) circle. Stack between sheets of waxed paper.

5. Heat ungreased heavy griddle or skillet over medium-high heat until a little water flicked on surface dances in tiny droplets. Carefully lay 1 tortilla on griddle; cook until top is bubbly and bottom is flecked with brown spots, 20 to 30 seconds.

6. Turn tortilla over; cook second side until speckled, 15 to 20 seconds. If tortilla puffs up while second side is cooking, press it down gently with spatula. Transfer to piece of aluminum foil.

7. Cook remaining tortillas as in Steps 5 and 6. Stack and cover with foil until all are cooked. Use immediately; or wrap in foil and keep warm in 250°F (120°C) oven up to 30 minutes. Tortillas can be refrigerated up to 3 days or frozen up to 2 weeks; reheat in 250°F (120°C) oven before using.
Makes 8 or 12 tortillas

Shredded Beef Tacos TACOS DE MACHACA

2 tablespoons (30 mL) lard or vegetable oil
1 pound (450 g) boneless beef chuck, cut into 1-inch (2.5-cm) cubes
1 to 2 teaspoons (5 to 10 mL) pure chili powder
1 clove garlic, minced
½ teaspoon (2 mL) salt
½ teaspoon (2 mL) ground cumin
1 can (14½ ounces or 410 g) whole peeled tomatoes, undrained, chopped
Vegetable oil
12 (6-inch or 15-cm) corn tortillas
1 cup (250 mL) shredded mild Cheddar cheese
2 to 3 cups (500 to 750 mL) shredded iceberg lettuce
1 large fresh tomato, seeded, chopped
Fresh coriander leaves

1. Heat lard in 10-inch (25-cm) skillet over medium-high heat until hot. Add beef; cook, turning frequently, until brown on all sides, 10 to 12 minutes. Reduce heat to low. Add chili powder, garlic, salt and cumin; cook and stir 30 seconds.

2. Add undrained canned tomatoes to skillet. Heat over

high heat to boiling; reduce heat to low. Simmer, covered, until beef is very tender, 1½ to 2 hours.

3. Using 2 forks, pull beef into coarse shreds in skillet. Cook beef mixture, uncovered, over medium heat, stirring frequently, until most of the liquid has evaporated and beef is moistly coated with sauce, 10 to 15 minutes. Keep warm.

4. Pour oil into deep, heavy skillet to depth of 1 inch (2.5 cm). Heat oil to 375°F (190°C); adjust heat to maintain temperature.

5. Fry tortillas in oil, 1 at a time, as follows: Fry tortilla a few seconds to soften. Using tongs, fold in half, holding slightly

open to leave space for filling; fry, turning occasionally, until crisp and golden, 1½ to 2 minutes. Drain on paper toweling.

6. Fill each taco shell with ¹⁄₁₂ of the beef, cheese, lettuce and fresh tomato, in that order. Garnish with coriander; serve immediately.

Makes 6 servings

Spiced Beef Enchiladas ENCHILADAS ROJAS

Red Chili Sauce (recipe follows)
1½ pounds (675 g) lean, boneless beef chuck, cut into 1-inch (2.5-cm) cubes
1 teaspoon (5 mL) salt
2 tablespoons (30 mL) lard or vegetable shortening
½ cup (125 mL) finely chopped white onion
¾ cup (180 mL) beef stock or broth
¼ cup (60 mL) raisins
1 clove garlic, minced
½ teaspoon (2 mL) ground cloves
¼ teaspoon (1 mL) anise seeds, crushed
12 (6-inch or 15-cm) corn tortillas
2 cups (500 mL) shredded mild Cheddar cheese
¾ cup (180 mL) Mexican Cream (see Index) or sour cream
⅓ cup (80 mL) sliced, pitted ripe olives
Chopped fresh coriander

1. Prepare Red Chili Sauce.

2. Sprinkle beef with salt. Heat lard in 10-inch (25-cm) skillet over medium-high heat until hot. Add ½ of beef and cook, turning frequently, until brown on all sides, 10 to 12 minutes; remove with slotted

spoon to plate. Repeat with remaining beef.

3. Add onion to drippings in skillet; saute over medium heat until soft, about 4 minutes. Return beef to skillet. Add stock, raisins, garlic, cloves, anise seeds and ¼ cup (60 mL) Red Chili Sauce; mix well. Heat over medium-high heat to boiling; reduce heat to low. Simmer, covered, stirring occasionally, until beef is very tender, 1½ to 2 hours.

4. Heat oven to 375°F (190°C). Using 2 forks, pull beef into coarse shreds in skillet. Heat remaining Chili Sauce in medium skillet over medium heat until hot; reduce heat to very low.

5. Dip 1 tortilla in hot sauce just until limp, a few seconds;

remove, draining off excess sauce. Spread about 3 tablespoons (45 mL) beef mixture down center of tortilla; roll up and place seam-side-down in 13×9×2-inch (33×23×5-cm) baking dish. Repeat with remaining tortillas and beef. Pour remaining sauce evenly over enchiladas.

6. Sprinkle enchiladas evenly with cheese. Bake until cheese is melted and sauce is bubbly, about 25 minutes. Just before serving, spoon Mexican Cream down center of enchiladas; garnish with olives and coriander.

Makes 4 to 6 servings

Red Chili Sauce

3 ounces (85 g) dried ancho chilies (about 5), toasted, seeded, deveined, rinsed

2½ cups (625 mL) boiling water
2 tablespoons (30 mL) vegetable oil
2 tablespoons (30 mL) tomato paste
1 clove garlic, minced
½ teaspoon (2 mL) salt
½ teaspoon (2 mL) dried oregano
¼ teaspoon (1 mL) ground cumin
¼ teaspoon (1 mL) ground coriander

1. Place chilies in medium bowl with boiling water; let stand 1 hour.

2. Transfer chilies and soaking water to blender container; process until smooth. Transfer puree to 2-quart (2-L) saucepan; whisk in remaining ingredients.

3. Heat over medium-high heat to boiling; reduce heat to very low. Simmer, covered, stirring occasionally, 10 minutes.

Makes about 2½ cups (625 mL)

Note: *Sauce can be refrigerated, covered, up to 3 days or frozen up to 1 month.*

Chicken & Black Bean Tostadas TOSTADAS DE POLLO

2 cups (500 mL) Refried *Black* Beans (see Index), cheese omitted
Fresh Tomato Salsa (see Index)
Lime-Cumin Dressing (recipe follows)
Vegetable oil
4 (10-inch or 25-cm) flour tortillas OR 8 (6-inch or 15-cm) corn tortillas
3 cups (750 mL) shredded cooked chicken
4 cups (1 L) shredded iceberg lettuce
1 small carrot, shredded
1 cup (250 mL) crumbled queso fresco or shredded mild Cheddar cheese
1 large firm-ripe avocado, pared, pitted, sliced
Pitted ripe olives
Radish slices
½ cup (125 mL) Mexican Cream (see Index) or sour cream, if desired

1. Prepare Refried Black Beans, mashing coarsely and omitting cheese.

2. Prepare Fresh Tomato Salsa.

3. Prepare Lime-Cumin Dressing.

4. Heat oven to 250°F (120°C). Pour oil into deep, heavy skillet (large enough to accommodate tortilla) to depth of 1 inch (2.5 cm). Heat oil to 375°F (190°C); adjust heat to maintain temperature.

5. Fry tortillas, 1 at a time, turning once, until crisp and light brown, about 30 seconds per side. Drain on paper toweling. Keep warm in oven on paper-towel-lined baking sheet.

6. Reheat beans, if necessary. Combine chicken, lettuce and carrot in large bowl. Add dressing; toss lightly to mix.

7. Place 1 flour or 2 corn tortillas on each serving plate. Spread beans on tortillas, dividing evenly. Sprinkle with ¾ cup (180 mL) cheese, dividing evenly. Top with chicken mixture and avocado.

8. Garnish tostadas with olives, radish slices and remaining ¼ cup (60 mL) cheese. Serve immediately with Fresh Tomato Salsa and Mexican Cream. **Makes 4 servings**

Lime-Cumin Dressing

2 tablespoons (30 mL) fresh lime juice
¼ teaspoon (1 mL) grated lime rind
¼ teaspoon (1 mL) salt
¼ teaspoon (1 mL) ground cumin
¼ cup (60 mL) vegetable oil

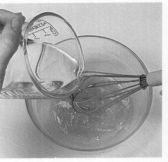

1. Combine lime juice, lime rind, salt and cumin in small bowl. Gradually add oil, whisking continuously, until thoroughly blended.
   Makes about ⅓ cup (80 mL)

Savory Pork Burritos BURRITOS DE CARNITAS

2 cups (500 mL) Refried Beans (see Index), cheese omitted
1 boneless fresh pork butt roast (about 2½ pounds or 1125 g)
1 cup (250 mL) chopped white onion
1 carrot, sliced
1 clove garlic, minced
1 teaspoon (5 mL) salt
½ teaspoon (2 mL) dried epazote
½ teaspoon (2 mL) ground cumin
½ teaspoon (2 mL) coriander seeds, lightly crushed
Water
Fresh Tomato Salsa (see Index)
12 (8-inch or 20-cm) flour tortillas
2 medium firm-ripe avocados, pared, pitted, diced
1 cup (250 mL) shredded Monterey Jack cheese
Carrot sticks
Green onions

1. Prepare Refried Beans, omitting cheese.

2. Place pork, onion, sliced carrot, garlic, salt, epazote, cumin and coriander seeds in 5- or 6-quart (5- or 6-L) Dutch oven. Add just enough water to cover pork. Heat over high heat to boiling; reduce heat to low. Simmer, covered, until pork is tender, 2 to 2½ hours.

3. Prepare Fresh Tomato Salsa.

4. Heat oven to 350°F (180°C). Remove pork from cooking liquid; strain and reserve ½ cup (125 mL) of the liquid.

5. Place pork on rack in roasting pan. Roast, turning once, until well-browned, 40 to 45 minutes.

6. Trim and discard outer fat from pork. Using 2 forks, pull pork into coarse shreds. Combine pork and reserved cooking liquid in medium skillet. Cook and stir over medium heat until pork is evenly moistened and hot, 3 to 5 minutes.

7. If not freshly made, soften and warm tortillas (see page 5). Reheat beans, if necessary.

8. For each burrito, place 1/12 of the beans crosswise in a row on lower half of 1 tortilla; spread out slightly. Top with 1/12 each pork, Tomato Salsa, avocado and cheese, in that order.

9. Fold right edge of tortilla over filling; fold bottom edge over filling and loosely roll up, leaving left end of burrito open.

10. Place 2 burritos on each serving plate. Garnish with carrot sticks and green onions; serve immediately.
    Makes 6 servings

Chicken in Oaxacan Black Mole POLLO EN MOLE NEGRO

3 small dried pasilla chilies
3 small dried mulato chilies
1½ cups (375 mL) boiling water
¼ cup (60 mL) sesame seeds
3 whole cloves
1-inch (2.5-cm) piece cinnamon stick
¼ teaspoon (1 mL) whole coriander seeds
⅛ teaspoon (0.5 mL) whole anise seeds
¼ cup (60 mL) lard or vegetable oil
¼ cup (60 mL) whole unblanched almonds
¼ cup (60 mL) raisins
6 whole chicken legs, thighs attached (about 3 pounds or 1350 g)
¼ teaspoon (1 mL) salt
½ cup (125 mL) coarsely chopped white onion
2 cloves garlic
1 tablespoon (15 mL) tomato paste
1½ ounces (45 g) Mexican chocolate, coarsely chopped
1 cup (250 mL) chicken stock or broth
Tomato wedges
Fresh coriander sprigs

1. Toast, seed, devein and rinse pasilla and mulato chilies (see page 5). Place in medium bowl with boiling water; let stand 1 hour.

2. Toast sesame seeds in dry heavy skillet over medium heat, stirring frequently, until golden, about 2 minutes. Remove from skillet. Combine cloves, cinnamon stick, coriander seeds and anise seeds in skillet; toast over medium heat, stirring frequently, until they start to change color and become fragrant, 20 to 30 seconds. Remove from skillet.

3. Heat lard in 12-inch (30-cm) skillet over medium heat until hot. Add almonds; cook and stir until brown, 2 to 3 minutes. Remove with slotted spoon;

drain on paper toweling. Add raisins; cook and stir until puffed, about 30 seconds. Remove with slotted spoon.

4. Sprinkle chicken with salt. Cook in lard over medium heat until brown, about 5 minutes per side; remove to plate. Remove all but 2 tablespoons (30 mL) lard from skillet.

5. Process raisins in blender until finely ground. Coarsely chop almonds; add to blender and process until finely ground. Add onion and garlic to blender; process until finely ground.

6. Process 2 tablespoons (30 mL) sesame seeds with on/ off pulses in electric spice grinder to fine powder; add to blender. Process clove mixture in grinder to fine powder; add to blender.

7. Add chilies, ⅓ cup (80 mL) of the soaking water and the tomato paste to blender; process until smooth. If mixture is too thick, add just as much remaining soaking water, 1 teaspoon (5 mL) at a time, needed to release blender blades.

8. Heat the lard in skillet over medium heat until hot; reduce heat to medium-low. Add chili mixture; cook, stirring constantly, 5 minutes. Add chocolate; cook and stir until melted, about 2 minutes. Gradually, stir in stock; cook, stirring frequently, 5 minutes.

9. Add chicken to skillet; reduce heat to low. Simmer, covered, turning occasionally, until tender, about 45 minutes. Place chicken on serving plates; top with sauce and remaining sesame seeds. Garnish with tomato wedges and coriander.

Makes 6 servings

Tablecloth-Stainer Chicken　MANCHA MANTELES DE POLLO

2 dried mulato chilies, toasted, seeded, deveined, rinsed (see page 5)
1 cup (250 mL) boiling water
2 small sweet potatoes (about ¾ pound or 340 g), pared
2 medium tomatoes, broiled (see page 5)
1 medium white onion, coarsely chopped
2 cloves garlic, chopped
¼ teaspoon (1 mL) ground cinnamon
2 tablespoons (30 mL) lard or vegetable oil
1 broiler-fryer chicken (3 to 3½ pounds or 1350 to 1600 g), cut into quarters
1 cup (250 mL) chicken stock or broth
1 cup (250 mL) cubed (¾-inch or 2-cm), pared fresh pineapple
1 tart apple, pared, cut into ½-inch (1.3-cm) cubes
¼ teaspoon (1 mL) salt, if desired
Fresh coriander sprigs
Bolillos (see Index), if desired
Lime wedges

1. Place chilies in small bowl with boiling water; let stand 1 hour.

2. Cut potatoes lengthwise into quarters; cut quarters crosswise into ½-inch (1.3-cm) thick slices.

3. Place chilies and ⅓ cup (80 mL) of the soaking water in blender container; discard remaining water. Add tomatoes, onion, garlic and cinnamon; process until smooth.

4. Heat lard in deep 10-inch (25-cm) skillet over medium heat until hot. Cook ½ chicken

at a time, turning occasionally, until brown on all sides, 10 to 15 minutes; remove chicken to plate. Remove and discard all but 2 tablespoons (30 mL) drippings from skillet.

5. Add chili mixture to skillet; cook, stirring constantly, over medium heat 5 minutes. Add stock; heat over high heat to boiling.

6. Add chicken, potatoes, pineapple and apple to skillet; simmer, covered, over low heat until chicken is tender, about 45 minutes. Remove chicken, potatoes and fruits to deep serving plates, dividing evenly; keep warm, covered.

7. Skim and discard fat from cooking liquid. Cook, stirring constantly, over medium-high heat until sauce is slightly thickened, 2 to 3 minutes. Stir in salt. Spoon sauce over chicken; garnish with coriander. Serve with Bolillos and lime wedges.

Makes 4 servings

Duckling in Pumpkin Seed Sauce　PATO EN PIPIAN

1 duckling (4½ to 5 pounds or 2 to 2.25 kg), cut into quarters
¼ teaspoon (1 mL) salt
2 tablespoons (30 mL) lard or vegetable oil
½ cup (125 mL) finely chopped white onion
3 fresh jalapeño chilies, seeded, finely chopped
2 cloves garlic, minced
8 small fresh (husked) or 1 cup (250 mL) drained canned tomatillos, finely chopped
½ cup (125 mL) fresh coriander leaves
⅓ cup (80 mL) shelled, roasted, salted pumpkin seeds
½ teaspoon (2 mL) ground cumin
½ teaspoon (2 mL) dried oregano
1 cup (250 mL) chicken stock
2 cups (500 mL) hot cooked rice, as accompaniment, if desired
Lime wedges
Radishes
Fresh coriander leaves

1. Cut off and discard wing tips of duck; remove and discard as much fat as possible.

2. Sprinkle duck with salt. Heat lard in 12-inch (30-cm) skillet over medium heat until hot. Add duck; cook until brown on both sides, about 5 minutes per side. Remove to plate.

3. Remove and discard all but 1 tablespoon (15 mL) drippings from skillet. Add onion, chilies and garlic; saute over medium heat until soft, about 3 min-

utes. Stir in tomatillos, ½ cup (125 mL) coriander, the pumpkin seeds, cumin and oregano.

4. Return duck to skillet; add stock. Heat to boiling; reduce heat to low. Simmer, covered, until duck is very tender, about 1 hour.

5. Heat oven to 400°F (200°C). Remove duck from skillet to baking sheet; place, uncovered, in oven while completing sauce.

6. Skim and discard fat from cooking liquid; process in blender until smooth. Return sauce to skillet; heat over medium heat, stirring frequently, to boiling.

7. Place duck on serving plates; add sauce. Serve with rice and lime, garnished with radishes and coriander.

Makes 4 servings

Almond Chicken POLLO ALMENDRADO

½ cup (125 mL) blanched almonds
3 whole chicken breasts (1 pound or 450 g each), split, boned, skinned
2 to 3 tablespoons (30 to 45 mL) vegetable oil
1 tablespoon (15 mL) butter or margarine
¼ cup (60 mL) finely chopped white onion
1 fresh Anaheim or poblano chili, roasted, peeled, seeded, deveined (see page 5), finely chopped
1 small tomato, seeded, finely chopped
1 clove garlic, minced
½ cup (125 mL) chicken stock or broth
¼ teaspoon (1 mL) salt
½ cup (125 mL) whipping cream
Tomato wedge
Fresh coriander sprig

1. Process almonds, about ¼ at a time, with on/off pulses in electric spice grinder to fine powder.

2. Dip chicken in almonds on small plate to coat all sides; reserve remaining almonds.

3. Heat 1 tablespoon (15 mL) oil and the butter in deep 10-inch (25-cm) skillet over medium heat until foam subsides. Add as many breasts as will fit in single layer without crowding. Cook until chicken is light brown on both sides,

about 3 minutes per side, reducing heat if almonds get too dark; remove to plate. Repeat with remaining chicken, adding 1 tablespoon (15 mL) oil, if needed.

4. Add remaining 1 tablespoon (15 mL) oil and the onion to skillet; saute over medium heat until soft, about 3 minutes.

Add chili, chopped tomato and garlic; saute 1 minute. Add stock, salt and reserved almonds; heat over high heat to boiling.

5. Add chicken to skillet; reduce heat to low. Simmer, covered, until chicken is cooked through, 15 to 20 minutes. Remove chicken to serving dish; keep warm, covered.

6. Add cream to cooking liquid; heat over medium-high heat to boiling. Cook and stir until sauce is slightly thickened, 3 to 5 minutes; pour over chicken. Garnish with tomato wedge and coriander.
Makes 6 servings

Broiled Chicken with Chili Butter PECHUGAS CON CHILE

⅓ cup (80 mL) Chili Butter (recipe follows)
3 whole chicken breasts (1 pound or 450 g each), split, boned
Fresh coriander sprigs

1. Prepare Chili Butter.

2. Cut Chili Butter crosswise into ⅛-inch (3-mm) thick

slices. Carefully loosen skin at 1 end of each chicken piece; insert 1 slice butter under skin.

3. Heat broiler. Place chicken, skin-side-down, on greased

rack in broiler pan; dot with some of the remaining butter. Broil chicken, 6 inches (15 cm) from heat source, until tops are brown, about 10 minutes. Turn

chicken over; dot with more of the remaining butter. Broil until skin is brown and juices run clear, not pink, when pierced with fork, about 10 minutes longer.

4. Place chicken on platter; top each piece with 1 slice butter. Serve, garnished with coriander.
Makes 6 servings

Chili Butter

1 small dried ancho chili, toasted, seeded, deveined, rinsed (see page 5)
1 cup (250 mL) boiling water
½ cup (125 mL) butter, at room temperature
1 clove garlic, minced
¼ teaspoon (1 mL) dried oregano

1. Place chili in small bowl with boiling water; let stand 1 hour.

2. Place chili and 1½ tablespoons (22 mL) of the soaking water in blender container; process until smooth. Cool completely. Discard remaining water.

3. Beat butter in small mixer bowl until fluffy. Beat in garlic and oregano. Gradually beat in chili to blend thoroughly. Refrigerate, covered, to firm slightly, about 30 minutes.

4. Spoon butter in a row onto plastic wrap; enclose in plastic and roll back and forth to form smooth 1-inch (2.5-cm) diameter roll. Refrigerate until firm, at least 1 hour.
Makes about ⅔ cup (160 mL)

Note: *Leftover Chili Butter can be frozen up to 1 month. Use on vegetables, rice, hamburgers, steaks and other grilled meats.*

Orange-Barbecued Chicken POLLO DORADO

1 or 2 dried de árbol chilies*
½ cup (125 mL) fresh orange
   juice
2 tablespoons (30 mL) tequila
2 cloves garlic, minced
1½ teaspoons (7 mL)
   shredded orange rind
½ teaspoon (2 mL) salt
¼ cup (60 mL) vegetable oil
1 broiler-fryer chicken (3 to
   3½ pounds or 1350 to
   1600 g), cut into quarters
Orange slices
Fresh coriander sprigs
Baked Green Rice (see
   Index), as accompaniment,
   if desired

*For milder flavor, seed chilies.

1. Crush chilies into coarse flakes in mortar with pestle.

2. Combine chilies, orange juice, tequila, garlic, orange rind and salt in small bowl. Gradually add oil, whisking continuously, until marinade is thoroughly blended.

3. Arrange chicken in single layer in shallow glass baking dish. Pour marinade over chicken; turn pieces to coat all sides: Refrigerate, covered, turning chicken over and brushing with marinade occasionally, 2 to 3 hours.

4. Prepare coals for charcoal fire (or heat broiler). Drain chicken, reserving marinade.

5. Grill (or broil) chicken, 6 to 8

inches (15 to 20 cm) from hot coals (or heat source), brushing frequently with reserved marinade, 15 minutes. Turn chicken over; continue cooking and brushing until chicken is cooked through, about 15 minutes longer.

6. Transfer chicken to serving dish; garnish with orange slices and coriander. Serve with Baked Green Rice.
Makes 4 servings

Turkey in Red Sesame Sauce GUAJOLOTE EN PIPIAN ROJO

1 boneless turkey breast half
   (about 4 pounds or 1800 g)
6 cups (1.5 L) turkey or
   chicken stock or broth
½ stalk celery
1 small white onion, cut in
   half
1 bay leaf
4 whole black peppercorns
4 dried ancho chilies
2 dried mulato chilies
2 cups (500 mL) boiling water
1¼ cups (310 mL) sesame
   seeds
3 cloves garlic
½-inch (1.3-cm) piece
   cinnamon stick
4 whole cloves
3 medium tomatoes, broiled
   (see page 5), cored
½ cup (125 mL) chopped
   white onion
¼ cup (60 mL) lard or
   vegetable oil
½ teaspoon (2 mL) salt
Fresh coriander sprigs

1. Tie turkey breast crosswise and lengthwise at 1½-inch (4-cm) intervals with kitchen string, folding thin ends under to make compact loaf.

2. Combine stock, celery, onion halves, bay leaf and peppercorns in 6-quart (6-L) Dutch oven; heat to boiling. Add turkey; reduce heat to very low. Simmer, partially covered, until turkey juices run clear when pierced to center, about 20 minutes per pound.

3. Meanwhile, prepare sauce. Seed, devein and rinse chilies; reserve seeds. Place chilies in medium bowl with boiling water; let stand 1 hour.

4. Toast sesame seeds in 10-inch (25-cm) dry skillet over medium heat, stirring frequently, just until light brown, 2 to 3 minutes; remove from skillet (cool seeds completely). Toast garlic, cinnamon, cloves and chili seeds in skillet over medium heat, stirring occasionally, until seeds are light brown and fragrant, 2 to 3 minutes; remove from skillet.

5. Process tomatoes, chopped onion and garlic in blender until very smooth. Drain chilies well; add to blender and process until very smooth.

6. Process sesame seeds in small batches with on/off pulses in electric spice grinder to fine powder; remove. (Do not overprocess or seeds will form paste.) Process chili seeds, cloves and cinnamon in grinder to powder.

7. Heat lard in 3-quart (3-L) saucepan over medium heat until hot. Add ground spices and seeds; cook, stirring constantly, until light brown, 2 to 3 minutes. (Do not allow to

burn.) Add tomato mixture; cook, stirring constantly, 5 minutes. Remove from heat.

8. Remove turkey from stock. Remove and discard string and skin; keep warm, covered. Strain stock; add 2 cups (500 mL) to sesame mixture. (Reserve remaining stock for other use.) Cook sauce, uncovered, over medium heat, stirring frequently, until thick enough to heavily coat spoon, about 10 minutes. Stir in salt.

9. To serve, cut turkey across grain into thin slices. Spoon about ½ cup (125 mL) sauce onto each serving plate; top with several turkey slices. Garnish with coriander.
Makes 6 to 8 servings

Pot Roast with Vegetables CARNE DE RES CON LEGUMBRES

2 tablespoons (30 mL) lard or vegetable oil
1 beef top round roast (about 3 pounds or 1350 g), tied
2 large white onions, cut into ⅜-inch (1-cm) thick slices
3 large cloves garlic, minced
3 cups (750 mL) beef stock or broth
4 dried pequín chilies or 1 dried seeded de árbol chili
½ teaspoon (2 mL) dried thyme
½ teaspoon (2 mL) dried oregano
2 pounds (900 g) fresh tomatillos, husked, or 2 cans (13 ounces or 370 g each) tomatillos, drained
2 large fresh poblano chilies, roasted, peeled, seeded, deveined (see page 5), cut into ½-inch (1.3-cm) wide strips
2 chayote squash
12 small red-skinned new potatoes, unpared
¼ cup (60 mL) minced fresh coriander

1. Heat lard in 5-quart (5-L) Dutch oven over medium heat until hot. Add beef; cook, turning occasionally, until brown on all sides, 10 to 15 minutes. Remove to plate.

2. Add onions and garlic to pan; saute over medium heat until soft, 6 to 8 minutes. Add stock, pequín chilies, thyme and oregano; heat over medium-high heat to boiling.

Add tomatillos to pan. If using fresh tomatillos, cook over medium heat until fork-tender, about 10 minutes.

3. Add beef to pan, pushing it down so it is surrounded by liquid. Place ¾ of poblano chili strips on top of beef. Heat over medium-low heat to simmering; simmer, partially covered, 2½ hours.

4. Pare and seed chayote; cut into 1×1½-inch (2.5×4-cm) pieces. Add chayote and potatoes to beef; simmer, covered, over medium-low heat until potatoes and beef are fork-tender, 30 to 40 minutes longer.

5. Remove beef, potatoes and chayote to warm serving platter; keep warm, covered. Process ½ the cooking sauce in blender at a time until smooth.

6. Return sauce to pan; cook over medium heat, stirring occasionally, until reduced to 4 cups (1 L), 20 to 25 minutes. Stir in coriander.

7. Garnish beef with remaining poblano chili strips. To serve, cut beef across grain into thin slices. Pass sauce separately.

Makes 6 to 8 servings

Tangy Braised Lamb Shanks CARNERO EN ADOBO

2 dried ancho chilies,
   toasted, seeded, deveined,
   rinsed (see page 5)
1 cup (250 mL) boiling water
2 tablespoons (30 mL) lard or
   vegetable oil
4 lamb shanks (about 1
   pound or 450 g each)
2 medium white onions, cut
   lengthwise into ⅛-inch
   (3-mm) thick slices
⅓ cup (80 mL) raisins
2 tablespoons (30 mL)
   piloncillo
3 cloves garlic, minced
¾ teaspoon (4 mL) dried
   oregano
½ teaspoon (2 mL) ground
   cumin
1 can (28 ounces or 800 g)
   whole peeled tomatoes,
   undrained, coarsely
   chopped
¾ cup (180 mL) beef stock
4 bay leaves
1 tablespoon (15 mL) cider
   vinegar
Shredded Romaine lettuce
Whole pitted ripe olives
Refried Beans (see Index), as
   accompaniment, if desired

1. Place chilies in small bowl with boiling water; let stand 1 hour.

2. Heat lard in 5- to 6-quart (5- to 6-L) Dutch oven over medium heat until hot; add 2 lamb shanks. Cook, turning occasionally, until brown on all sides, about 20 minutes; remove to plate. Repeat with remaining shanks.

3. Place chilies and ⅓ cup (80 mL) of the soaking liquid in blender container; process until smooth. Discard remaining soaking liquid.

4. Remove and discard all but 2 tablespoons (30 mL) drippings from Dutch oven. Add onions; saute over medium heat until soft, about 4 minutes. Reduce heat to medium-low. Stir in raisins, piloncillo, garlic, oregano and cumin. Add chili puree; cook and stir 2 minutes.

5. Add tomatoes, stock and bay leaves to pan; heat over high heat to boiling. Add lamb shanks; reduce heat to low. Simmer, covered, turning occasionally, until lamb is very tender, 2 to 2½ hours.

6. Remove lamb to serving plates; keep warm. Skim and discard fat from cooking sauce; stir in vinegar. Heat sauce over medium-high heat to boiling; cook, uncovered, stirring frequently, until sauce is thickened, about 10 minutes. Spoon sauce over lamb. Serve, garnished with lettuce and olives, accompanied by Refried Beans.

Makes 4 servings

Veal in Walnut Sauce TERNERA EN NOGADA

2 pounds (900 g) boneless
   veal shoulder, cut into
   1-inch (2.5-cm) cubes
2 cups (500 mL) veal or
   chicken stock
1 small white onion, cut into
   quarters
2 cloves garlic
½ teaspoon (2 mL) dried
   thyme
1½ cups (375 mL) Mexican
   Cream (see Index) or
   whipping cream
1¼ cups (310 mL) walnuts
¼ cup (60 mL) sliced
   blanched almonds
2 tablespoons (30 mL) lard or
   vegetable oil
¼ cup (60 mL) minced white
   onion
½ cup (125 mL) minced fresh
   coriander
¼ teaspoon (1 mL) salt
Radishes
Fresh coriander sprigs
2 to 3 cups (500 to 750 mL)
   hot cooked white rice, as
   accompaniment, if desired
1 to 1½ pounds (450 to 675 g)
   cooked green beans, as
   accompaniment, if desired

1. Combine veal, stock, quartered onion, garlic and thyme in 3-quart (3-L) saucepan. Heat over medium-high heat to boil-

ing; reduce heat to low. Simmer, partially covered, until veal is fork-tender, about 1 hour.

2. Meanwhile, combine Mexican Cream, 1 cup (250 mL) walnuts and the almonds in small saucepan. Heat over medium-low heat to simmering; cook 5 minutes. Remove from heat; let stand 30 minutes.

3. Toast remaining ¼ cup (60 mL) walnuts in small dry skillet over medium heat, turning occasionally, until golden, 2 to 3 minutes. Reserve.

4. Drain veal, reserving stock. Discard onion and garlic.

5. Transfer cream mixture to blender container. Process until very smooth. Add reserved stock; process until blended.

6. Heat lard in deep 10-inch (25-cm) skillet over medium heat until hot. Add minced onion; saute until soft, about 4 minutes. Add veal; saute 5

minutes. Stir in cream sauce; heat to simmering. Simmer, uncovered, stirring occasionally, until sauce is slightly thickened, about 15 minutes.

7. Stir minced coriander and salt into veal mixture. Serve, garnished with toasted walnuts, radishes and coriander sprigs, accompanied by rice and green beans.

Makes 4 to 6 servings

Pork with Green Chilies CHILE VERDE

2 tablespoons (30 mL) lard or vegetable oil
3 pounds (1350 g) lean, fresh boneless pork butt, cut into 1½-inch (4-cm) cubes
2 medium white onions, thinly sliced lengthwise
3 cloves garlic, minced
1½ teaspoons (7 mL) salt
1 teaspoon (5 mL) ground cumin
¾ teaspoon (4 mL) dried oregano
8 small fresh (husked) or 1 cup (250 mL) drained canned tomatillos, finely chopped
3 or 4 fresh Anaheim chilies or canned green chilies, seeded, deveined, finely chopped
1 large tomato, peeled, coarsely chopped
¼ cup (60 mL) fresh coriander leaves
¾ cup (180 mL) chicken stock or broth
2 teaspoons (10 mL) lime juice
4 cups (1 L) hot cooked white rice

½ cup (125 mL) toasted slivered almonds
Fresh coriander sprigs
Radish slices

1. Heat lard in 5- to 6-quart (5- to 6-L) Dutch oven over medium heat until hot. Add about ⅓ of pork in single layer. Cook, turning occasionally, until brown on all sides, about 10 minutes; remove to plate. Repeat until all pork has been browned.

2. Remove and discard all but 2 tablespoons (30 mL) drippings from pan. Add onions and garlic; saute over medium heat un-

til soft, about 4 minutes. Stir in salt, cumin and oregano.

3. Add tomatillos, chilies, tomato and coriander leaves to pan; stir in stock. Heat over high heat to boiling.

4. Return pork to pan; reduce heat to low. Simmer, covered, until pork is tender, 1½ to 2 hours.

5. Uncover pan; increase heat to medium. Cook at low boil, stirring occasionally, until sauce is thickened, 20 to 30 minutes longer. Stir in lime juice.

6. To serve, spoon pork mixture over rice; sprinkle with almonds. Garnish with coriander sprigs and radish slices.
Makes 6 to 8 servings

Ribs in Orange & Chili Sauce COSTILLITAS EN NARANJA

2 tablespoons (30 mL) lard or vegetable oil
4 pounds (1800 g) country-style spareribs, cut into individual ribs
2 medium white onions, cut lengthwise into ¼-inch (6-mm) wide slivers
1 can (1 pound or 450 g) whole peeled tomatoes, undrained
2 cloves garlic
1 to 2 tablespoons (15 to 30 mL) ground, seeded, dried ancho chilies
½ teaspoon (2 mL) ground cinnamon
¼ teaspoon (1 mL) ground cloves
½ cup (125 mL) fresh orange juice
⅓ cup (80 mL) dry white wine
¼ cup (60 mL) piloncillo
1 teaspoon (5 mL) shredded orange rind
½ teaspoon (2 mL) salt
1 to 2 tablespoons (15 to 30 mL) cider vinegar

Orange slices, cut into halves
Fresh coriander sprigs
1½ pounds (675 g) cooked baby carrots, as accompaniment, if desired

1. Heat lard in 5- or 6-quart (5- or 6-L) Dutch oven over medium heat until hot. Add as many ribs as will fit in single layer without crowding. Cook, turning occasionally, until brown on all sides, 15 to 20 minutes; remove to plate. Repeat with remaining ribs.

2. Remove and discard all but 2 tablespoons (30 mL) drippings from pan. Add onions; saute over medium heat until soft, about 4 minutes.

3. Quickly process tomatoes and garlic in blender container until smooth.

4. Add chilies, cinnamon and cloves to onions; cook and stir over medium heat 30 seconds. Add tomato mixture; cook and stir 5 minutes.

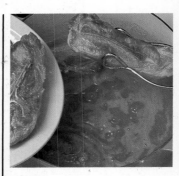

5. Add orange juice, wine, piloncillo, orange rind and salt to pan; heat over high heat to boiling. Add ribs; reduce heat to low. Simmer, covered, until ribs are tender, about 1½ hours.

6. Remove ribs to serving plates. Skim and discard fat from cooking sauce. Stir in vinegar; spoon sauce over ribs. Serve, garnished with orange slices and coriander, accompanied by carrots.
Makes 4 to 6 servings

Picadillo-Stuffed Chilies   CHILES RELLENOS DE PICADILLO

Tomato Sauce (recipe follows)
OR Mexican Cream (see
Index) and chopped
fresh coriander
8 fresh poblano or Anaheim
chilies
Picadillo Filling (recipe
follows)
Vegetable oil
⅓ cup (80 mL) all-purpose
flour
5 large eggs, separated, at
room temperature
¼ teaspoon (1 mL) cream of
tartar
¼ teaspoon (1 mL) salt

1. Prepare Tomato Sauce.

2. Roast, peel, seed and devein chilies (see page 5), leaving stems intact and taking care not to break chilies.

3. Prepare Picadillo Filling.

4. Carefully spoon about ¼ cup (60 mL) Filling into each chili; press chilies firmly between hands to ease out air and to close.

5. Heat oven to 250°F (120°C). Pour oil into deep, heavy, large skillet to depth of 1 inch (2.5 cm). Heat over medium heat to 365°F (185°C); adjust heat to maintain temperature.

6. Roll each chili in flour to coat lightly; pat off excess. Reserve remaining flour (about ¼ cup or 60 mL).

7. Beat egg whites, cream of tartar and salt in large mixer bowl until soft peaks form. Beat egg yolks in medium

mixer bowl until thick and lemon colored; gradually beat in reserved flour until smooth. Fold ¼ of egg whites into yolk mixture; fold in remaining egg whites until blended.

8. Fry 2 or 3 chilies at a time in oil as follows: Grasp stem; support bottom of chili with fork. Dip into batter to coat; let excess drain off. Slip chili into oil; fry, turning once, until deep gold, about 2 minutes per side. Remove with slotted spatula; drain on paper toweling. Keep warm in oven until all have been fried.

9. Reheat Tomato Sauce until hot; divide evenly among 4 deep serving plates. Top each with 2 chilies; serve immediately. (OR pass Mexican Cream, sprinkled with coriander.)   **Makes 4 servings**

Tomato Sauce

1½ pounds (675 g) tomatoes,
peeled, seeded
1 medium white onion,
chopped
1 clove garlic, chopped
2 tablespoons (30 mL) lard or
vegetable oil
1½ cups (375 mL) chicken
stock or broth
¼ teaspoon (1 mL) dried
thyme
¼ teaspoon (1 mL) salt

1. Place tomatoes, onion and garlic in blender container; process until smooth.

2. Heat lard in deep 10-inch (25-cm) skillet over medium heat until hot. Add tomato mixture; cook and stir 5 minutes.

3. Stir stock, thyme and salt into skillet. Heat over high heat to boiling; reduce heat to medium-low. Cook, stirring frequently, until sauce is slightly thickened, 10 to 15 minutes. Remove from heat.
Makes about 2 cups (500 mL)

Picadillo Filling

1 tablespoon (15 mL)
vegetable oil
¼ cup (60 mL) slivered
almonds
¾ pound (340 g) ground beef
chuck
¼ cup (60 mL) finely
chopped white onion
1 large tomato, peeled,
seeded, finely chopped
1 tablespoon (15 mL) tomato
paste
1 clove garlic, minced
2 tablespoons (30 mL) raisins
2 tablespoons (30 mL) thinly
sliced, pimiento-stuffed
green olives
1 tablespoon (15 mL) cider
vinegar
1 teaspoon (5 mL) piloncillo
¼ teaspoon (1 mL) salt
¼ teaspoon (1 mL) ground
cinnamon
⅛ teaspoon (0.5 mL) ground
cumin
⅛ teaspoon (0.5 mL) ground
cloves

1. Heat oil in 10-inch (25-cm) skillet over medium heat until

hot. Add almonds; cook and stir until golden, 2 to 3 minutes. Remove with slotted spoon; drain on paper toweling.

2. Crumble beef into skillet; cook over medium heat, breaking up beef into small pieces, until no longer red, about 5 minutes. Add onion; saute until onion is soft, about 4 minutes. Add tomato, tomato paste and garlic; saute 2 min-

utes. Stir in remaining ingredients; reduce heat to low. Simmer, covered, 15 minutes.

3. Uncover skillet; increase heat to medium-low. Cook until most of the liquid has evaporated, about 3 minutes. Skim and discard fat. Stir in almonds; let stand, uncovered, just until cool enough to handle.
Makes about 2 cups (500 mL)

Variation: Cheese-Stuffed Chilies. Prepare as above, except for Picadillo Filling substitute 3 tablespoons (45 mL) of the following mixture in each chili: 1½ cups (375 mL) shredded queso Chihuahua or Monterey Jack cheese, 2 fresh husked and minced tomatillos and 3 thinly sliced green onions.

Skirt Steak Ranchero CARNE ASADA

2 beef skirt steaks (about 1 pound or 450 g each)
2 cloves garlic
3 tablespoons (45 mL) vegetable oil
2 tablespoons (30 mL) plus 1 to 2 teaspoons (5 to 10 mL) fresh lime juice
Pinch ground black pepper
½ cup (125 mL) minced white onion
2 large tomatoes, seeded, diced (⅜ inch or 1 cm)
2 small green bell peppers, roasted, peeled, seeded, deveined (see page 5), diced (⅜ inch or 1 cm)
2 tablespoons (30 mL) minced fresh coriander
1 fresh serrano chili, minced
Refried Beans (see Index), as accompaniment, if desired
Skillet Red Rice (see Index), as accompaniment, if desired

1. Place steaks between pieces of heavy plastic; pound with flat side of meat mallet to ¼-inch (6-mm) thickness. Cut crosswise into halves.

2. Pound 1 clove garlic with mallet to crush into coarse shreds; combine with 2 tablespoons (30 mL) each oil and lime juice and the black pepper in large, shallow, nonmetal baking dish. Add steaks, turning to coat both sides with marinade. Let stand, covered, at room temperature, turning occasionally, 30 minutes.

3. Mince remaining garlic clove. Saute onion and garlic in remaining 1 tablespoon (15 mL) oil in medium skillet over medium heat until soft, 3 to 4 minutes; remove from heat.

4. Stir tomatoes, bell peppers, coriander and chili into onion mixture. Add remaining 1 to 2 teaspoons (5 to 10 mL) lime juice to taste. Let relish stand, covered, at room temperature.

5. Prepare coals for charcoal fire.* Remove steaks from marinade; pat dry with paper toweling. Grill 6 inches (15 cm)

from coals, turning once, until desired doneness, about 1½ minutes per side for medium-rare.

6. Transfer steaks to warm plates; spoon relish along side of each serving. Accompany with Refried Beans and Skillet Red Rice.

Makes 4 to 6 servings

Steaks can be cooked on lightly oiled, well-seasoned heavy griddle or large skillet; heat over medium heat until very hot. Cook steaks in single layer on griddle, about 1½ minutes per side.

Stuffed Meatballs ALBONDIGAS EN SALSA DE CHIPOTLE

2 large eggs
1 teaspoon (5 mL) salt
⅓ cup (80 mL) packaged fine dry breadcrumbs
1½ pounds (675 g) lean ground beef
½ pound (225 g) ground pork
¼ cup (60 mL) coarsely chopped fresh coriander
9 (¾-inch or 2-cm) cubes queso fresco (about 3½ ounces or 100 g)
9 whole pimiento-stuffed green olives
2 tablespoons (30 mL) lard or vegetable oil
1 cup (250 mL) finely chopped white onion
2 cloves garlic, minced
1 can (1 pound or 450 g) whole peeled tomatoes, undrained, coarsely chopped
½ cup (125 mL) beef stock or broth
2 to 4 canned chipotle chilies in adobo sauce, finely chopped
Sliced pimiento-stuffed olives

1. Beat eggs with salt in large bowl. Stir in breadcrumbs; let stand 5 minutes. Add beef, pork and coriander; mix lightly but thoroughly.

2. Divide meat mixture into 18 even portions. Shape 1 portion into flat patty; top with 1 cheese cube. Press meat firmly around cheese to enclose completely and form ball. Repeat procedure, stuffing ½ of meat portions with cheese and ½ with whole olives.

3. Heat lard in deep 10-inch (25-cm) skillet over medium heat until hot. Fry ½ of meatballs at a time, turning occasionally, until brown on all sides, about 5 minutes; remove to plate.

4. Remove and discard all but 3 tablespoons (45 mL) drippings from skillet. Add onion and garlic; saute over medium heat until soft, about 4 minutes. Stir in tomatoes, stock and chilies; heat to boiling.

5. Return meatballs to skillet; reduce heat to low. Simmer, covered, until meatballs are cooked through, about 45 minutes. Remove meatballs to serving dish with slotted spoon; keep warm.

6. Transfer tomato mixture to blender container; process until smooth. Return mixture to skillet; heat over high heat to boiling. Pour sauce over and around meatballs. Serve with sliced olives.

Makes 4 to 6 servings

Border-Style Chili

2 tablespoons (30 mL) lard or
   vegetable oil
2 pounds (900 g) ground
   chuck, coarse chili grind*
2 cups (500 mL) finely
   chopped white onion
1 or 2 dried de árbol or
   japonés chilies
2 cloves garlic, minced
1 to 1½ teaspoons (5 to
   7 mL) salt
1 teaspoon (5 mL) ground
   cumin
¼ teaspoon (1 mL) ground
   cloves
1 can (28 ounces or 800 g)
   whole peeled tomatoes,
   undrained, coarsely
   chopped
½ cup (125 mL) fresh orange
   juice
½ cup (125 mL) tequila or
   water
¼ cup (60 mL) tomato paste
1 tablespoon (15 mL) grated
   orange rind
Lime wedges
Fresh coriander sprigs

*If butcher cannot coarsely grind
meat, use regular ground chuck.

1. Heat lard in deep 12-inch (30-cm) skillet over medium-high heat until hot. Crumble beef into skillet; cook, stirring frequently, until beef is no longer red, 6 to 8 minutes. Add onion; saute over medium heat until onion is soft, about 5 minutes.

2. Crush chilies into fine flakes in mortar with pestle. Add chilies, garlic, salt, cumin and cloves to skillet. Cook and stir 30 seconds.

3. Add tomatoes, orange juice, tequila, tomato paste and orange rind to skillet; mix well. Heat over high heat to boiling; reduce heat to low. Simmer, covered, stirring occasionally, 1½ hours.

4. Uncover skillet. Cook chili, stirring frequently, over medium-low heat until slightly thickened, 10 to 15 minutes. Serve, garnished with lime wedges and coriander sprigs.
Makes 4 to 6 servings

Chili-Barbecued Pork   CECINA ENCHILADA OAXAQUENA

3 tablespoons (45 mL)
   ground, seeded, dried
   pasilla chilies
1 teaspoon (5 mL) coarse or
   Kosher salt
½ teaspoon (2 mL) ground
   cumin
2 tablespoons (30 mL)
   vegetable oil
1 tablespoon (15 mL) fresh
   lime juice
3 cloves garlic, minced
2 pounds (900 g) pork
   tenderloin or thick
   boneless loin pork chops,
   trimmed of fat
Shredded Romaine lettuce
Radishes and/or radish slices
Refried *Black* Beans (see
   Index), as accompaniment,
   if desired

1. Mix chilies, salt and cumin in small bowl. Stir in oil and lime juice to make smooth paste. Stir in garlic.

2. Butterfly pork by cutting lengthwise about ⅔ of the way

through, leaving meat in one piece; spread meat flat. Cut tenderloin crosswise into 8 equal pieces (do not cut chops into pieces).

3. Place pork between sheets of heavy plastic; pound with flat side of meat mallet to ¼-inch (6-mm) thickness.

4. Spread chili paste on both sides of pork pieces to coat evenly. Place in shallow glass baking dish. Refrigerate, covered, 2 to 3 hours.

5. Prepare coals for charcoal fire or heat broiler. Grill or broil pork 6 inches (15 cm) from heat source, turning once, until brown on outside and cooked through (no longer pink) in center, 4 to 5 minutes per side for grill or about 3 minutes per side for broiler. Serve, garnished with lettuce and radishes, accompanied by Refried Black Beans.
Makes 4 to 6 servings

Red Snapper Veracruz HUACHINANGO A LA VERACRUZANA

6 red snapper fillets (8 to 10 ounces or 225 to 285 g each)
¼ teaspoon (1 mL) salt
⅛ teaspoon (0.5 mL) pepper
⅓ cup (80 mL) all-purpose flour
¼ cup (60 mL) olive oil
3 cloves garlic, sliced
2 medium white onions, cut lengthwise into thin slivers
1½ pounds (675 g) fresh plum tomatoes, peeled, seeded, finely chopped
½ cup (125 mL) tomato juice
¼ cup (60 mL) fresh lime juice
¼ cup (60 mL) sliced pimiento-stuffed green olives
1 or 2 pickled jalapeño chilies, seeded, finely chopped
1 tablespoon (15 mL) drained capers
1 bay leaf
3 pounds (1350 g) cooked small red-skinned potatoes, cut into halves
Chopped fresh coriander

1. Sprinkle fish with salt and pepper. Dip in flour to coat both sides; shake off excess.

2. Heat oil in 12-inch (30-cm) skillet over medium heat until hot. Add garlic; cook, stirring

frequently, until golden, 2 to 3 minutes. Remove garlic with slotted spoon and discard.

3. Add as many fillets to skillet as will fit in single layer without crowding. Cook over medium heat, turning once, until

light brown, about 2 minutes per side; remove to plate. Repeat with remaining fillets.

4. Add onions to skillet; saute over medium heat until soft, about 4 minutes. Stir in tomatoes, tomato juice, lime juice, olives, chilies, capers and bay leaf. Heat over high heat to boiling; reduce heat to low. Simmer, covered, 15 minutes.

5. Add any juices which have collected from fish on plate to skillet. Cook sauce, uncovered, over medium-high heat, stirring frequently, until thickened, 2 to 3 minutes. Remove and discard bay leaf.

6. Add fish to skillet. Spoon sauce over fish; reduce heat to low. Simmer, covered, just until fish are opaque throughout, 3 to 5 minutes. Serve immediately with potatoes, garnished with coriander.

Makes 6 servings

Marinated Skewered Fish BROCHETA DE PESCADO MARINADA

1 chayote squash*
2 quarts (2 L) boiling water
¼ cup (60 mL) minced fresh
    coriander
3 tablespoons (45 mL) fresh
    lime juice
1 or 2 fresh jalapeño chilies,
    seeded, deveined, minced
1 clove garlic, minced
¼ teaspoon (1 mL) dried
    oregano
⅛ teaspoon (0.5 mL) salt
⅛ teaspoon (0.5 mL) freshly
    ground black pepper
½ cup (125 mL) olive oil
1 pound (450 g) mackerel
    fillets or swordfish, shark
    or halibut steaks
2 or 3 fresh güero chilies**
4 or 5 large green onions
16 cherry tomatoes

*If unavailable, substitute 2 small
zucchini. Do not pare; cut into
½-inch (1.3-cm) thick slices. In
Step 2, decrease cooking time to 2
to 3 minutes.

**Any mild or sweet pepper, such
as banana, cubanelle or bell pepper,
can be substituted.

1. Place 6 to 8 long wooden skewers in warm water to soak.

2. Pare and seed chayote; cut into 1¼-inch (3-cm) pieces. Add chayote to boiling water in medium saucepan; cook over medium heat, just until crisp-tender, 3 to 5 minutes. Drain chayote; immediately rinse under cold running water. Drain well.

3. Combine coriander, lime juice, jalapeños, garlic, oregano, salt and black pepper in medium bowl. Gradually add oil, whisking continuously, until marinade is thoroughly blended.

4. Cut fish into 1½-inch (4-cm) squares, removing any bones.

Add fish and chayote to marinade; mix well. Let stand, covered, at room temperature, 20 to 30 minutes.

5. Prepare coals for charcoal grilling or heat broiler. Seed and devein güero chilies; cut

into 1-inch (2.5-cm) squares. Cut onions into 1½-inch (4-cm) lengths.

6. Drain fish and chayote, reserving marinade. Thread fish, chayote, chilies, onions and tomatoes alternately onto skewers.

7. Grill or broil 6 inches (15 cm) from heat source, turning and basting frequently with marinade, until fish is opaque throughout and vegetables are tender, about 6 minutes. Serve immediately with any remaining marinade.

Makes 4 to 6 servings

Shrimp in Pumpkin Seed Sauce CAMARONES EN PIPIAN VERDE

2 pounds (900 g) fresh
    medium shrimp, in shells
1 quart (1 L) water
½ teaspoon (2 mL) salt
2 whole black peppercorns
8 ounces (225 g) shelled,
    unsalted raw pumpkin
    seeds
½ cup (125 mL) minced fresh
    coriander
1 small white onion, cut into
    quarters
2 fresh jalapeño chilies,
    roasted, peeled, seeded,
    deveined (see page 5)
1 clove garlic
2 tablespoons (30 mL) butter
    or margarine
1 cup (250 mL) Mexican
    Cream (see Index) or
    whipping cream
Fresh coriander sprigs

1. Shell and devein shrimp, reserving shells. Refrigerate shrimp, covered.

2. Combine shrimp shells, the water, salt and peppercorns in large saucepan. Heat to boil-

ing; reduce heat to low. Simmer, partially covered, 20 minutes; strain shrimp broth.

3. Return broth to pan; heat over medium-low heat to simmering. Add shrimp; cook just until opaque throughout, 2 to 3 minutes. Drain, reserving broth; refrigerate shrimp, covered.

4. Toast pumpkin seeds in dry 10-inch (25-cm) skillet over medium heat, stirring constantly, just until seeds begin to pop, 3 to 5 minutes; do not

allow to brown. Immediately transfer to plate; cool completely.

5. Process seeds in small batches with on/off pulses in electric spice grinder to fine

powder. Combine ground seeds, shrimp broth, ¼ cup (60 mL) minced coriander, the onion, chilies and garlic in blender container; process until very smooth.

6. Heat butter in large saucepan over medium heat until hot. Add broth mixture; cook, stirring frequently, until sauce

thickens enough to coat spoon, 10 to 15 minutes.

7. Stir Mexican Cream into sauce. Heat to boiling; reduce heat to medium. Simmer, stirring frequently, 5 minutes. Stir in remaining ¼ cup (60 mL) minced coriander.

8. Reserve 12 shrimp for garnish. Add remaining shrimp to sauce; cook over low heat, stirring occasionally, just until heated through, 2 to 3 minutes. Serve immediately, garnished with reserved shrimp and coriander sprigs.

Makes 4 to 6 servings

58

Sole with Papaya PESCADO CON PAPAYA

1 firm-ripe papaya (1 to 1¼ pounds or 450 to 565 g)
1 pound (450 g) fresh skinless sole or pompano fillets
¼ cup (60 mL) fresh lime juice
¼ teaspoon (1 mL) salt
⅓ cup (80 mL) all-purpose flour
¼ cup (60 mL) butter or margarine
1 tablespoon (15 mL) vegetable oil
⅛ teaspoon (0.5 mL) ground cinnamon
1 tablespoon (15 mL) piloncillo

1. Cut papaya lengthwise in half; scoop out seeds and discard. Pare papaya; cut lengthwise into ½-inch (1.3-cm) thick slices.

2. Sprinkle fish with 1 tablespoon (15 mL) lime juice; let stand 5 minutes.

3. Sprinkle fish with salt. Place flour on waxed paper. Dip fish in flour to coat both sides; shake off excess.

4. Heat 2 tablespoons (30 mL) butter and the oil in 12-inch (30-cm) skillet over medium-high heat until foamy. Add as many fish fillets as will fit in single layer without crowding. Cook, turning once, until golden on outside and opaque throughout, 1½ to 2 minutes per side. Remove to warm serving platter; keep warm. Repeat with any remaining fillets.

5. Add remaining 2 tablespoons (30 mL) butter to skillet; heat over medium heat until bubbly. Add papaya;

sprinkle with cinnamon. Cook, turning papaya over gently, just until heated through, about 1 minute. Remove papaya with slotted spatula; arrange on platter with fish.

6. Sprinkle piloncillo over drippings in skillet; stir to mix. Stir in remaining 3 tablespoons (45 mL) lime juice. Heat over medium-high heat to boiling; cook and stir until sauce is slightly thickened, 1 to 1½ minutes. Spoon sauce over fish and serve immediately.
Makes 3 to 4 servings

Mayan Fish PESCADO MAYA

1 cup (250 mL) boiling water
1 tablespoon (15 mL) annatto seeds
1½ tablespoons (22 mL) orange juice
1½ tablespoons (22 mL) cider vinegar
2 cloves garlic, chopped
1 small dried de árbol chili, coarsely crumbled
¾ teaspoon (4 mL) ground cumin
½ teaspoon (2 mL) ground allspice
¼ teaspoon (1 mL) salt
⅛ teaspoon (0.5 mL) pepper
4 pieces fresh halibut steaks or mackerel or sea bass fillets (about 8 ounces or 225 g each)
Vegetable oil
Sliced green onions

1. Pour boiling water over annatto seeds in small bowl; let stand, covered, at room temperature, until soft, 8 to 10 hours or overnight.

2. Drain annatto seeds. Combine seeds, orange juice, vinegar, garlic, chili, cumin, allspice, salt and pepper in blender container; process until smooth.

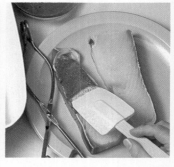

3. Spread annatto paste over fish to coat both sides. Place fish in single layer in well-oiled baking dish. Refrigerate, covered, to blend flavors, 1 to 2 hours.

4. Heat oven to 350°F (180°C). Bake fish, uncovered, until opaque throughout, 20 to 25 minutes. Sprinkle with green onions; serve immediately.
Makes 4 servings

Shrimp in Fiery Garlic Butter   CAMARONES EN MOJO DE AJO

1½ pounds (675 g) fresh
    medium shrimp, in shells
½ cup (125 mL) butter
¼ cup (60 mL) vegetable oil
8 cloves garlic, finely
    chopped
1 to 3 dried de árbol chilies,
    coarsely crumbled*
1 tablespoon (15 mL) fresh
    lime juice
¼ teaspoon (1 mL) salt
Green onion tops, slivered
Bolillos (see Index) or crusty
    French bread

*For milder flavor, seed some or all
chilies.

1. Heat oven to 400°F (200°C).
Shell and devein shrimp, leaving tails attached; rinse and
drain well.

2. Combine butter and oil in 8-
to 9-inch (20- to 23-cm) skillet;
heat over medium heat until
butter is melted and foamy.
Add garlic, chilies, lime juice
and salt; cook and stir 1 minute. Remove from heat.

3. Spread shrimp in even layer
in shallow 2-quart (2-L) gratin
pan or baking dish or in 4 shallow 2-cup (500-mL) gratin
pans. Pour hot butter mixture
over shrimp.

4. Bake shrimp, stirring once
or twice, just until opaque
throughout and sizzling hot,
10 to 12 minutes. (Do not over-
cook or shrimp will be dry and
tough.) Garnish with green onions; serve immediately. Use
Bolillos to blot up butter sauce.
Makes 4 servings

Fish Fillets in Green Sauce   PESCADO REBOZADO EN SALSA VERDE

¼ cup (60 mL) vegetable oil
¼ cup (60 mL) chopped
    white onion
1 or 2 fresh jalapeño chilies,
    seeded, finely chopped
1 cup (250 mL) husked,
    chopped fresh tomatillos
    or drained, small canned
    tomatillos
2 cloves garlic, minced
¼ teaspoon (1 mL) ground
    cumin
⅓ cup (80 mL) plus 1
    tablespoon (15 mL) water
⅓ cup (80 mL) coarsely
    chopped fresh coriander
½ teaspoon (2 mL) salt
⅓ cup (80 mL) all-purpose
    flour
⅛ teaspoon (0.5 mL) pepper
1 large egg
2 tablespoons (30 mL) butter
    or margarine
1½ to 2 pounds (675 to 900 g)
    small red snapper fillets
    or skinless sole fillets
Lime slices
Fresh coriander sprig
Lime wedges

1. Heat 2 tablespoons (30 mL)
oil in 8- to 9-inch (20- to 23-cm)
skillet over medium heat until
hot. Add onion and chilies;
saute until soft, about 4 minutes. Add tomatillos, garlic and
cumin; saute 1 minute.

2. Add ⅓ cup (80 mL) water,
the chopped coriander and ¼
teaspoon (1 mL) salt to skillet.
Heat over high heat to boiling;
reduce heat to low. Simmer,
covered, 20 minutes. Transfer
mixture to blender container;

process until smooth. Return
sauce to skillet; reserve, off
heat.

3. Mix flour, remaining ¼ teaspoon (1 mL) salt and the pepper on plate. Beat egg with 1
tablespoon (15 mL) water in
shallow bowl.

4. Heat butter and remaining 2
tablespoons (30 mL) oil in
12-inch (30-cm) skillet over
medium-high heat until foamy.
Working with as many fillets as
will fit in skillet in single layer,
quickly dip each fillet in flour to
coat both sides lightly; shake

off excess. Dip in egg; let excess
drain off. Add to skillet; cook
over medium-high heat, turning once, until light brown on
outside and opaque at center of
thickest point, 2 to 4 minutes
per side. Remove to serving
platter; keep warm. Repeat
with remaining fillets.

5. Quickly heat reserved sauce
over medium heat, stirring frequently, until hot. Pour over
and around fish; garnish with
lime slices and coriander sprig.
Serve immediately with lime
wedges.
Makes 4 to 6 servings

Pork Tamales in Banana Leaves TAMALES CON PUERCO

1 pound (450 g) boneless pork shoulder, cut into ½-inch (1.3-cm) cubes
3 cups (750 mL) water
1 very small white onion, cut in half
2 cloves garlic
1 pound (450 g) fresh tomatillos, husks removed*
Boiling water
3 fresh poblano chilies, roasted, peeled, seeded, deveined (see page 5)
10 small Romaine lettuce leaves
3 sprigs fresh coriander
3 tablespoons (45 mL) chopped white onion
7½ tablespoons (112 mL) lard or vegetable shortening, at room temperature
2 cups (500 mL) masa harina
1½ teaspoons (7 mL) salt
1½ teaspoons (7 mL) baking powder
4 or 5 banana leaves**
Large Romaine lettuce leaves, if desired
Tomato wedges

*If unavailable, substitute 1 can (13 ounces or 370 g) tomatillos, drained; omit Step 2.

**Banana leaves are available in Mexican groceries and some florists; aluminum foil can be substituted.

1. Place pork, 3 cups (750 mL) water, the onion halves and 1 clove garlic in medium saucepan. Heat over medium heat to boiling; reduce heat to low. Simmer, partially covered, until pork is fork-tender, 20 to 30 minutes. Drain pork, reserving 1½ cups (375 mL) broth.

2. Place tomatillos and boiling water to cover in medium saucepan. Simmer over medium heat until fork-tender, 8 to 10 minutes; drain.

3. Place tomatillos, chilies, 2 small lettuce leaves, the coriander, chopped onion and remaining clove garlic in blender container; process until smooth.

4. Heat 2 tablespoons (30 mL) lard in 4-quart (4-L) saucepan over medium heat until hot; add tomatillo mixture. Cook and stir until slightly thick-

ened, 3 to 4 minutes. Stir in pork; simmer, stirring occasionally, until pork is very tender, 20 to 30 minutes.

5. Mix masa harina, salt and baking powder in medium bowl. Beat remaining 5½ tablespoons (82 mL) lard in large mixer bowl until light and fluffy, 5 to 10 minutes. Beat in masa mixture, ¼ cup (60 mL) at a time; beat until thoroughly blended. Heat reserved pork broth just until warm; gradually beat into masa mixture to form soft, moist dough.

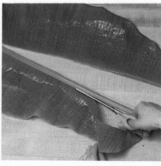

6. Rinse banana leaves well; using scissors, cut out and discard center rib. Cut leaf halves crosswise into 8-inch (20-cm) squares; you will need about 24 squares. Set gas or electric burner at medium heat. Pass

each leaf square quickly across burner a few times until pliable; do not overheat or it will become brittle.

7. Cut remaining 8 small lettuce leaves crosswise into halves. Spread about 2 tablespoons (30 mL) dough into a 3-inch (8-cm) square on center of 1 banana-leaf piece. Top with about 2 tablespoons (30 mL) pork mixture; cover with ½ lettuce leaf. Fold sides,

then ends, of banana leaf over filling to enclose. Repeat to make 16 tamales.

8. Line large steamer basket with remaining 8 banana leaf squares. Stack tamales in basket, folded sides down; cover with kitchen towel.

9. Place steamer basket over 3 to 4 inches (8 to 10 cm) boiling water; cover with lid. Adjust heat to maintain gentle boil; steam tamales until dough is cooked through, about 1 hour. Transfer to serving bowl lined with large lettuce leaves; garnish with tomato. Serve hot.

Makes 4 servings

Savory Chicken Tamales TAMALES CON POLLO

60 to 70 dried corn husks
Hot water
2 tablespoons (30 mL) lard or vegetable oil
1 cup (250 mL) finely chopped white onion
¼ cup (60 mL) sesame seeds
½ teaspoon (2 mL) ground cinnamon
1 clove garlic, minced
1 can (1 pound or 450 g) whole peeled tomatoes, undrained, coarsely chopped
1 can (7 ounces or 200 g) chipotle chilies in adobo sauce*
½ cup (125 mL) water
1 broiler-fryer chicken (about 3 pounds or 1350 g), cut up
2 teaspoons (10 mL) salt
1 cup (250 mL) lard or vegetable shortening, at room temperature
3 cups (750 mL) masa harina
1¾ to 2 cups (435 to 500 mL) warm chicken stock or broth
Boiling water

Chipotle chilies are very hot; for milder flavor, use ½ can and sauce.

1. Place corn husks in large pot; add very hot water to cover. Top husks with plate and heavy jar to keep submerged. Let stand at least 3 hours or overnight.

2. Heat 2 tablespoons (30 mL) lard in deep 10-inch (25-cm) skillet over medium heat until hot. Add onion and sesame seeds; saute until onion is soft and seeds are golden, about 4 minutes. Stir in cinnamon and garlic; add tomatoes, chilies and ½ cup (125 mL) water.

3. Add chicken to skillet; sprinkle with 1 teaspoon (5 mL) salt. Heat over high heat to boiling; reduce heat to low. Simmer, covered, until chicken is very tender, about 1 hour. Remove chicken with tongs to plate; let stand until cool enough to handle.

4. Skim and discard fat from tomato mixture; cook over medium-high heat, stirring occasionally, until reduced to 3 cups (750 mL), 8 to 10 minutes. Transfer to blender container; process until smooth.

5. Remove and discard skin and bones from chicken; cut into ⅜- to ½-inch (1- to 1.3-cm) cubes.

6. Drain corn husks; rinse and rub each husk under running water to remove any silk and debris. Drain well; pat dry. Wrap in towel to keep pliable.

7. Beat 1 cup (250 mL) lard in large mixer bowl until light and fluffy, 5 to 10 minutes. Beat in masa harina, ¼ cup (60 mL) at a time; beat until thoroughly blended. Beat in remaining 1 teaspoon (5 mL) salt. Gradually beat in stock, using just as much needed to form dough that just holds together.

8. For each tamale, spread heaping tablespoon dough in center of 1 corn husk to form 3-inch (8-cm) square. Top with about 2 teaspoons (10 mL) tomato mixture and 4 to 6 chicken cubes.

9. Fold right, then left edges of husk over filling. Fold wide end of husk over filled area; fold pointed end over and tuck into center of folded wide end. Turn tamale seam-side-down. Make 50 tamales in all.

10. Line large steamer basket with remaining corn husks. Stack tamales in basket, seam-sides-down. Cover tamales with kitchen towel.

11. Place steamer basket over 3 to 4 inches (8 to 10 cm) boiling water; cover with lid. Adjust heat to maintain gentle boil. Steam tamales about 40 minutes. Remove 1 tamale from center of basket and carefully unwrap; if dough pulls easily away from husk, it is done. If necessary, steam 5 or 10 minutes longer and test again. Serve tamales hot.

Makes 6 to 8 servings

Sweet Pineapple Tamales TAMALES DE DULCE

40 to 50 dried corn husks
Hot water
¾ cup (180 mL) firmly packed crushed piloncillo
¼ cup (60 mL) lard or vegetable shortening, at room temperature
¼ cup (60 mL) butter or margarine, at room temperature
½ teaspoon (2 mL) vanilla
2 cups (500 mL) masa harina
½ teaspoon (2 mL) ground cinnamon
¼ teaspoon (1 mL) ground nutmeg
Pinch salt
¾ to 1 cup (180 to 250 mL) warm water
⅓ cup (80 mL) flaked coconut
⅓ cup (80 mL) raisins

2 cups (500 mL) diced fresh pineapple
Boiling water
2 cups (500 mL) Mexican Cream (see Index) or sour cream

1. Soak and clean corn husks according to directions in Steps 1 and 6 of Savory Chicken Tamales (see above).

2. Combine piloncillo, lard and butter in large mixer bowl; beat until light and fluffy, 5 to 10 minutes. Beat in vanilla. Mix masa harina, cinnamon, nutmeg and salt in medium bowl. Beat masa harina mixture into butter mixture, ¼ cup (60 mL) at a time; beat until thoroughly

blended. Gradually beat in warm water, using just as much needed to form dough that just holds together. Stir in coconut and raisins.

3. For each tamale, spread rounded tablespoon dough in center of 1 corn husk to form

3-inch (8-cm) square; top with 4 to 6 pineapple pieces. Make 30 tamales in all.

4. Fold tamales, place in steamer basket and steam according to directions in Steps 9, 10 and 11 of Savory Chicken Tamales (see above). Serve tamales hot with Mexican Cream.

Makes about 6 servings

Note: *Sweet tamales are most often served for breakfast or mid-morning snack with hot chocolate, but can be served as dessert after a light meal, if desired.*

Egg Dishes

Ranch-Style Eggs HUEVOS RANCHEROS

2 to 4 fresh serrano chilies*
1 large clove garlic
4 medium tomatoes (about 1½ pounds or 675 g), peeled, seeded
¾ cup (180 mL) plus 2 tablespoons (30 mL) vegetable oil
⅓ cup (80 mL) finely chopped white onion
½ teaspoon (2 mL) salt
¼ teaspoon (1 mL) sugar
¼ teaspoon (1 mL) ground cumin
8 (6-inch or 15-cm) corn tortillas
8 large eggs
⅓ cup (80 mL) crumbled queso fresco
1 firm-ripe avocado, pitted, pared, sliced
Fresh coriander sprigs

*For milder flavor, seed some or all of the chilies.

1. Combine chilies and garlic in blender container; process until finely chopped. Add tomatoes; process until finely chopped (but not pureed).

2. Heat 2 tablespoons (30 mL) oil in medium skillet over medium heat until hot. Add onion; saute until soft, about 4 minutes. Add tomato mixture, salt, sugar and cumin; cook over medium-high heat, stirring frequently, until sauce thickens slightly, 6 to 8 minutes. Keep warm.

3. Heat oven to 250°F (120°C). Heat remaining ¾ cup (180 mL) oil in 10-inch (25-cm) skillet over medium heat until hot. Fry tortillas in oil, 1 at a time, just until limp and blistered, 5 to 10 seconds per side. (Tortillas can be fried a little longer, until slightly crisp, if desired.) Drain well on paper toweling; keep warm in oven.

4. Remove all but 2 tablespoons (30 mL) oil from skillet. Fry 4 eggs at a time over medium-low heat until whites are set, but yolks are still soft, 2 to 3 minutes.

5. Arrange 2 tortillas on each serving plate; place 1 egg on each tortilla. Top with sauce; sprinkle with cheese. Garnish with avocado and coriander; serve immediately.
Makes 4 servings

Mexican Potato Omelet TORTILLA DE PATATAS

1 large red-skinned potato,
  scrubbed
8 large eggs
2 tablespoons (30 mL) cold
  water
¼ teaspoon (1 mL) salt
Pinch black pepper
2 tablespoons (30 mL) lard or
  vegetable oil
¾ cup (180 mL) finely
  chopped white onion
½ red or green bell pepper,
  seeded, finely chopped
1 or 2 fresh jalapeño chilies,
  seeded, minced
¼ cup (60 mL) crumbled
  queso añejo
2 tablespoons (30 mL) minced
  fresh coriander
Tomato wedges

1. Cut potato into ⅜-inch
(1-cm) cubes.

2. Lightly whisk eggs, water,
salt and black pepper in medium bowl.

3. Heat lard in 10-inch (25-cm)
nonstick skillet or omelet pan*
over medium heat until hot.
Add potato, onion and bell
pepper; saute until potato is
tender, about 6 minutes. Stir in
chilies.

4. Pour egg mixture into skillet;
cook over medium heat, stirring with back of fork, just until

bottom starts to set, 1 or 2 minutes. Cook, lifting up edges,
tilting pan and letting un-
cooked egg mixture flow to
bottom, 1 or 2 minutes longer.
Cook without stirring or lifting, until top is set and bottom
is golden, about 1 minute
longer.

5. Sprinkle omelet with cheese
and coriander. Garnish with
tomato. Cut omelet into 4 or 8
wedges; serve immediately.
Makes 4 servings

*If nonstick pan is unavailable, use
well-seasoned, heavy skillet.*

Scrambled Eggs, Mexican Style HUEVOS REVUELTOS A LA MEXICANA

8 large eggs
¾ teaspoon (4 mL) salt
2 tablespoons (30 mL) butter
  or margarine
2 tablespoons (30 mL)
  vegetable oil
⅓ cup (80 mL) finely
  chopped white onion
2 to 4 fresh serrano chilies,
  finely chopped*
2 medium tomatoes, seeded,
  chopped, drained
Fresh coriander sprigs
Warm corn tortillas, if
  desired
Fresh fruit, if desired

*Fresh chilies provide crunchy tex-
ture which cannot be duplicated
with canned chilies. For milder
flavor, seed some or all of the
chilies.*

1. Lightly whisk eggs and salt
in medium bowl.

2. Heat butter and oil in
10-inch (25-cm) skillet over
medium heat until hot. Add
onion and chilies; saute until
hot, but not soft, 45 seconds.

3. Stir tomatoes into onion
mixture; increase heat to
medium-high. Cook and stir
until tomatoes are very hot, 45
seconds.

4. Add egg mixture all at once
to skillet; cook without stirring
1 minute. Continue cooking,
stirring lightly, until eggs are
softly set, 2 to 3 minutes longer.
Garnish with coriander. Serve
immediately with tortillas and
fruit.

Makes 4 servings

Salads & Side Dishes

Jícama Salad ENSALADA DE JICAMA

1 jícama (1¼ to 1½ pounds
    or 565 to 675 g)*
1 small cucumber, unpared
½ cup (125 mL) very thinly
    slivered mild red onion
2 tablespoons (30 mL) fresh
    lime juice
½ teaspoon (2 mL) grated
    lime rind
1 clove garlic, minced
¼ teaspoon (1 mL) salt
⅛ teaspoon (0.5 mL)
    crumbled dried de árbol
    chili
3 tablespoons (45 mL)
    vegetable oil
Leaf lettuce

*If unavailable, substitute Jeru-
salem artichokes. Cut pared artichokes lengthwise into halves; cut
halves crosswise into thin slices.

1. Pare jícama; cut lengthwise
into 8 wedges; cut wedges
crosswise into ⅛-inch (3-mm)
thick slices.

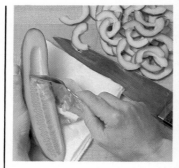

2. Cut cucumber lengthwise in
half; scoop out and discard
seeds. Cut halves crosswise
into ⅛-inch (3-mm) thick
slices.

3. Combine jícama, cucumber
and onion in large bowl; toss
lightly to mix.

4. Mix lime juice, lime rind,
garlic, salt and chili in small
bowl. Gradually add oil,
whisking continuously, until
dressing is thoroughly
blended.

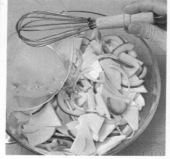

5. Pour dressing over jícama
mixture; toss lightly to coat. Refrigerate, covered, 1 to 2 hours
to blend flavors before serving.

6. To serve, line shallow salad
bowl with lettuce leaves.
Spoon salad on top of lettuce.
Makes 6 servings

Sliced Avocado Salad ENSALADA DE AGUACATE

1 tablespoon (15 mL) cider vinegar
1 tablespoon (15 mL) fresh orange juice
1 teaspoon (5 mL) grated orange rind
¼ teaspoon (1 mL) salt
Pinch pepper
3 tablespoons (45 mL) olive oil
3 fresh plum tomatoes (about ½ pound or 225 g), seeded, finely chopped
¼ cup (60 mL) coarsely chopped fresh coriander
2 tablespoons (30 mL) finely chopped mild red onion
1 fresh jalapeño chili, seeded, finely chopped
2 large firm-ripe avocados
2 cups (500 mL) shredded iceberg lettuce
Fresh coriander sprigs

1. Mix vinegar, orange juice, orange rind, salt and pepper in medium bowl. Gradually add oil, whisking continuously, until dressing is thoroughly blended.

2. Add tomatoes, chopped coriander, onion and chili to dressing; toss lightly to mix. Let stand, covered, at room temperature up to 2 hours to blend flavors before serving.

3. Just before serving, cut avocados lengthwise into halves; remove and discard pits. Pare avocados; cut lengthwise into ½-inch (1.3-cm) thick slices.

4. Spread ½ cup (125 mL) lettuce on each of 4 chilled salad plates. Arrange avocado over lettuce, dividing evenly; top with tomato mixture, dividing evenly. Garnish with coriander sprigs.

Makes 4 servings

Marinated Zucchini Salad ENSALADA DE CALABACITAS

3 medium zucchini (about 6 ounces or 170 g each)
½ teaspoon (2 mL) salt
5 tablespoons (75 mL) white vinegar
1 clove garlic, minced
¼ teaspoon (1 mL) dried thyme
½ cup (125 mL) olive oil
1 cup (250 mL) drained canned garbanzo beans (chick peas)
½ cup (125 mL) sliced, pitted ripe olives
3 green onions, minced
1 canned chipotle chili in adobo sauce, drained, seeded, minced
1 ripe avocado, pitted, pared, cut into ½-inch (1.3-cm) cubes
⅓ cup (80 mL) crumbled queso añejo OR 3 tablespoons (45 mL) grated Romano cheese
1 head Boston lettuce, cored, separated into leaves

1. Cut zucchini lengthwise into halves; cut halves crosswise into ¼-inch (6-mm) thick slices. Place slices in medium bowl; sprinkle with salt. Toss to mix. Spread zucchini on several layers of paper toweling; let stand at room temperature 30 minutes to drain.

2. Combine vinegar, garlic and thyme in large bowl. Gradually

add oil, whisking continuously, until dressing is thoroughly blended.

3. Pat zucchini dry; add to dressing. Add beans, olives and onions; toss to coat with dressing. Refrigerate, covered, stirring occasionally, at least 30 minutes or up to 4 hours.

4. Just before serving, add chili to salad; stir gently to distribute evenly. Add avocado and cheese; toss lightly to mix.

5. To serve, line shallow bowl or platter with lettuce; top with zucchini mixture.

Makes 4 to 6 servings

Skillet Red Rice ARROZ A LA MEXICANA

2 tablespoons (30 mL) lard or vegetable oil
1 cup (250 mL) raw long-grain white rice (not converted)
½ cup (125 mL) finely chopped white onion
1 clove garlic, minced
½ teaspoon (2 mL) salt
½ teaspoon (2 mL) ground cumin
Pinch pure hot chili powder
2 large tomatoes, peeled, seeded, chopped
1½ cups (375 mL) chicken stock or broth
⅓ cup (80 mL) shelled fresh or thawed frozen peas
2 tablespoons (30 mL) chopped pimiento
Pimiento strips

1. Heat lard in 10-inch (25-cm) skillet over medium heat until hot. Add rice; cook, stirring constantly, until rice turns opaque white, about 2 minutes.

2. Quickly add onion; saute over medium heat 1 minute. Stir in garlic, salt, cumin and chili powder. Add tomatoes; cook, stirring constantly, 2 minutes.

3. Add stock; mix well. Heat over high heat to boiling; reduce heat to low. Simmer, covered, until rice is almost tender, about 15 minutes.

4. Stir in peas and chopped pimiento. Cook, covered, over low heat until rice is tender and all liquid has been absorbed, 2 to 4 minutes longer. Rice grains will be slightly firm (al dente) and separate, rather than soft or sticky. Serve, garnished with pimiento strips.
    Makes 4 to 6 servings

Baked Green Rice ARROZ VERDE

2 tablespoons (30 mL) lard or vegetable oil
1 cup (250 mL) raw long-grain white rice (not converted)
¼ cup (60 mL) finely chopped white onion
2 fresh poblano or Anaheim chilies, roasted, peeled, seeded, deveined (see page 5), chopped
6 thin green onions, thinly sliced
1 clove garlic, minced
¼ teaspoon (1 mL) salt
¼ teaspoon (1 mL) ground cumin
1¾ cups (430 mL) chicken stock or broth
1½ cups (375 mL) shredded queso Chihuahua
⅓ cup (80 mL) coarsely chopped fresh coriander
Fresh coriander sprig

1. Heat oven to 375°F (190°C). Heat lard in 10-inch (25-cm) skillet over medium heat until hot. Add rice; cook, stirring constantly, until rice turns opaque white, about 2 minutes.

2. Quickly add white onion; saute over medium heat 1 minute. Add chilies, green onions, garlic, salt and cumin; saute 20 seconds.

3. Add stock; mix well. Heat over high heat to boiling; reduce heat to low. Simmer, covered, until rice is almost tender, about 15 minutes.*

4. Remove skillet from heat. Add 1 cup (250 mL) cheese and

the chopped coriander; toss lightly to mix. Transfer to greased 1½-quart (1.5-L) baking dish; top with remaining cheese.

5. Bake, uncovered, until rice is tender and cheese topping is melted, about 15 minutes. Garnish with coriander sprig.
    Makes 4 to 6 servings

For plain green rice, complete recipe from this point as follows: Continue cooking rice in skillet until tender, 2 to 4 minutes longer. Stir in chopped coriander just before serving; omit cheese.

Baked Stuffed Zucchini CALABACITAS RELLENAS

3 medium zucchini (6 ounces or 170 g each)
3 quarts (3 L) water
3 tablespoons (45 mL) unsalted butter
¼ cup (60 mL) minced white onion
1 clove garlic, minced
1¼ cups (310 mL) fresh or frozen corn kernels
2 fresh poblano chilies, roasted, peeled, seeded, deveined (see page 5), chopped
½ cup (125 mL) shredded queso Chihuahua or Monterey Jack cheese
2 tablespoons (30 mL) minced fresh coriander
¼ teaspoon (1 mL) salt
Pinch pepper
Fresh coriander sprigs

1. Cut zucchini lengthwise into halves; scoop out pulp, leaving ¼-inch (6-mm) thick shells. Chop pulp; reserve.

2. Heat the water in large saucepan over high heat to boiling. Add zucchini shells; simmer over medium-high heat 3 minutes. Drain and immediately rinse under cold running water. Invert shells on several layers paper toweling to drain well.

3. Heat butter in 10-inch (25-cm) skillet over medium heat until hot. Add onion and garlic; saute until soft, about 3

minutes. Add zucchini pulp; saute 1 minute. Add corn and chilies; saute until corn is crisp-tender, about 3 minutes. Remove from heat; let stand until slightly cool, about 10 minutes.

4. Heat oven to 350°F (180°C). Add cheese, minced coriander, salt and pepper to corn mixture; mix well. Spoon into zucchini shells, dividing evenly. Place shells in buttered, shallow baking dish. Bake until vegetables are heated through and cheese is melted, 15 to 20 minutes. Serve, garnished with coriander sprigs.
Makes 6 servings

Tomato Variation: Substitute 6 medium firm-ripe tomatoes for zucchini. Slice off and discard stem ends; scoop out, chop and drain insides, leaving ½-inch (1.3-cm) thick tomato shells. Omit Step 2; invert shells on paper toweling to drain well. Proceed with recipe as above.

Chayote with Onions CHAYOTE CON CEBOLLAS

2 chayote squash (1½ to 2 pounds or 675 to 900 g total)*
2 medium white onions
2 tablespoons (30 mL) butter or margarine
1 tablespoon (15 mL) vegetable oil
½ teaspoon (2 mL) dried oregano
¼ to ½ teaspoon (1 to 2 mL) salt
Pinch pepper

*Zucchini or kohlrabi can be substituted for chayote. For zucchini, decrease cooking time in Step 5 to 3 to 5 minutes. For kohlrabi, increase cooking time in Step 5 to 12 to 15 minutes.

1. Pare and seed chayotes; cut lengthwise into ½-inch (1.3-cm) thick slices.

2. Cut onions lengthwise into halves. Cut halves lengthwise into ¼-inch (6-mm) thick slices; separate into slivers.

3. Heat butter and oil in 10-inch (25-cm) skillet over medium heat until foam subsides. Add onions and oregano; saute over medium-low heat until onions are golden, 8 to 10 minutes.

4. Add chayote to skillet; saute over medium heat, 3 minutes.

5. Cover skillet; reduce heat to low. Cook until chayote is crisp-tender, 8 to 10 minutes. Stir in salt and pepper.
Makes 4 to 6 servings

Chuckwagon Beans FRIJOLES A LA CHARRA

¾ pound (340 g) dried red or
pink beans (2 cups or
500 mL)
5 cups (1250 mL) cold water
1 smoked ham hock or
smoked pork neck bone
(about ¾ pound or 340 g)
¼ cup (60 mL) lard or
vegetable oil
1 large white onion, finely
chopped
2 tablespoons (30 mL) tomato
paste
2 cloves garlic, minced
1 to 3 fresh jalapeño or
serrano chilies, seeded,
finely chopped
½ to 1 teaspoon (2 to 5 mL)
salt
¼ cup (60 mL) coarsely
chopped fresh coriander
Corn Tortilla Chips (see
Index), if desired

1. Rinse beans thoroughly in
sieve under cold running
water, picking out any debris or
blemished beans.

2. Combine beans, water and
ham hock in 4- or 5-quart (4- or
5-L) Dutch oven. Heat over
high heat to boiling; reduce
heat to very low. Simmer, covered, just until beans are tender but not soft, about 1½
hours.

3. Heat lard in medium skillet
over medium heat until hot.
Add onion; saute until soft,

about 4 minutes. Add tomato
paste, garlic and chilies; cook
and stir 30 seconds.

4. Add onion mixture and salt
to beans; cook, covered, over

low heat, stirring frequently,
until beans are soft, about 30
minutes.

5. Remove ham hock to plate;
let stand until cool enough to
handle. Remove meat from
bone; chop meat and add to
beans.

6. Heat beans until very hot.
Just before serving, stir in coriander; serve with Corn Tortilla Chips.
Makes 6 to 8 servings

Refried Beans FRIJOLES REFRITOS

8 ounces (225 g) dried red,
pink, pinto or black
beans* (1⅓ cups or
330 mL)
4½ cups (1125 mL) cold
water
⅓ cup (80 mL) plus 1
tablespoon (15 mL) lard or
vegetable oil
1 small white onion, sliced
1½ teaspoons (7 mL) salt
1 small white onion, finely
chopped
1 small clove garlic, minced
¼ cup (60 mL) queso fresco
Romaine lettuce
Radishes
Corn Tortilla Chips (see
Index), if desired

*If using black beans, add ½ tea-
spoon (2 mL) dried epazote with
salt in Step 3.

1. Rinse beans thoroughly in
sieve under cold running
water, picking out any debris or
blemished beans.

2. Combine beans, water, 1 tablespoon (15 mL) lard and the
sliced onion in 3-quart (3-L)
heavy saucepan. Heat over
high heat to boiling; reduce
heat to very low. Simmer, covered, just until beans are tender but not soft, about 1½
hours.

3. Stir salt into beans; continue
cooking, covered, over very
low heat until beans are very
soft, 30 to 45 minutes longer.
Do not drain.**

4. Heat remaining ⅓ cup (80
mL) lard in heavy 10-inch (25-
cm) skillet over high heat until
very hot. Add chopped onion
and garlic; saute over medium
heat until soft, about 4
minutes.

5. Increase heat to high. Immediately add 1 cup (250 mL)
undrained beans; cook and stir
while mashing beans with
bean masher or potato masher.

6. As beans begin to dry, add
another 1 cup (250 mL) beans;
continue mashing and cooking. Repeat until all beans and
cooking liquid have been

added and mixture is coarse
puree. Adjust heat as needed
to prevent beans from sticking
and burning; total cooking
time will be about 20 minutes.

7. Transfer beans to serving
dish; sprinkle with cheese.
Garnish with lettuce and radishes; serve with Corn Tortilla
Chips.
**Makes about 2 cups (500 mL);
4 to 6 servings**

**Flavor is improved if beans are
prepared to this point, then refrigerated, covered, overnight before
completing recipe.

Easter Egg Bread PAN DE PASCUA

1 cup (250 mL) milk
⅔ cup (160 mL) sugar
¼ cup (60 mL) butter or
    margarine
¼ cup (60 mL) lard or
    vegetable shortening
1 teaspoon (5 mL) salt
2 packages (¼ ounce or 7 g
    each) active dry yeast
½ cup (125 mL) warm water
    (105 to 115°F or 40 to 46°C)
5 to 5½ cups (1250 to
    1375 mL) all-purpose flour
3 large egg yolks
1 teaspoon (5 mL) vanilla
1 large egg white
1 tablespoon (15 mL) cold
    water
¼ cup (60 mL) raisins
3 tablespoons (45 mL) diced
    mixed candied fruits
Egg Filling (recipe follows)
2 tablespoons (30 mL) sesame
    seeds

1. Scald milk in small saucepan over medium heat; remove from heat. Add sugar, butter, lard and salt; stir until butter and lard are melted. Let stand at room temperature until lukewarm, about 10 minutes.

2. Sprinkle yeast over the warm water in small bowl; stir to mix. Let stand 5 minutes.

3. Combine milk and yeast mixtures in large mixer bowl; add 2½ cups (625 mL) flour. Mix at low speed; then beat at medium speed until smooth. Let stand, covered, in warm place until bubbly, about 20 minutes.

4. Beat egg yolks and vanilla into batter. Add 1½ cups (375 mL) flour; mix at low speed, then beat at medium speed until smooth and elastic, about 3 minutes. Gradually stir in as much of the remaining flour needed to make soft dough, about 1 cup (250 mL).

5. Knead dough on floured surface, adding just as much remaining flour as needed to prevent sticking, until smooth and elastic, about 15 minutes. Place in greased bowl; turn dough over to grease top. Let rise, covered, in warm place until doubled, about 1 hour.

6. Beat egg white and cold water lightly in small bowl. Punch down dough. Pinch off ¼ of the dough (about 1 cup or 250 mL); reserve. Knead raisins into remaining dough; shape dough into ball. Place on greased baking sheet; flatten to make ½-inch (1.3-cm) thick circle, about 10 inches (25 cm) in diameter. Brush lightly with egg white.

7. Divide reserved dough into 24 equal pieces. Roll each into 5-inch (13-cm) long strand; shape each into "S." Arrange in 2 rings on outer portion of dough circle. Decorate border with candied fruits.

8. Let bread rise, loosely covered, in warm place until almost doubled, about 45 minutes.

9. Heat oven to 350°F (180°C). Prepare Egg Filling.

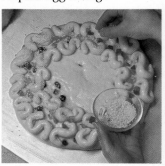

10. Brush dough again with egg white. Sprinkle with sesame seeds. Bake 30 minutes, covering border design with small pieces of foil when gold-

en to prevent burning. Spoon Egg Filling onto center. Bake until bread is brown and sounds hollow when tapped, 8 to 10 minutes longer. Carefully remove from baking sheet; cool on wire rack.
        **Makes 13-inch (33-cm)
        round loaf**

Egg Filling

1 large egg
2 tablespoons (30 mL) sugar
1 tablespoon (15 mL) all-
    purpose flour
½ teaspoon (2 mL) vanilla

1. Beat egg in small mixer bowl until thick and pale yellow. Beat in sugar, flour and vanilla until blended.

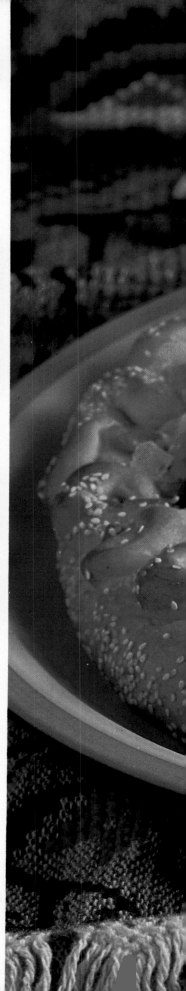

Mexican Doughnut Strips CHURROS

1 cup (250 mL) water
½ cup (125 mL) butter or margarine
1 teaspoon (5 mL) sugar
¼ teaspoon (1 mL) salt
¼ teaspoon (1 mL) ground nutmeg
1 cup (250 mL) all-purpose flour
4 large eggs, at room temperature
½ teaspoon (2 mL) vanilla
Vegetable oil
⅓ cup (80 mL) sugar

1. Combine water, butter, 1 teaspoon (5 mL) sugar, the salt and nutmeg in 2-quart (2-L) saucepan. Heat over medium-high heat, stirring occasionally, until butter is melted. Increase heat to high; heat to full rolling boil.

2. Add flour to pan all at once; immediately remove from heat

and beat with wooden spoon until mixture forms smooth, thick paste. Cook and stir over medium-high heat until mixture pulls away from sides of pan to form ball and begins to form film on bottom of pan, 1 to 2 minutes. Remove from heat.

3. Add eggs, 1 at a time, beating vigorously after each addition until dough is smooth and shiny. Stir in vanilla. Let dough stand at room temperature 15 minutes.

4. Pour oil into deep, heavy, large skillet to depth of 1 inch (2.5 cm). Heat to 375°F (190°C); adjust heat to maintain temperature.

5. Spoon dough into pastry bag or cookie press fitted with large (about ½-inch or 1.3-cm) star tip.

6. Carefully press dough directly into hot oil in 6-inch (15-cm) long strips, cutting strips with scissors to detach. Fry 3 or 4 strips at a time, turning once, until brown, 2½ to 3½ minutes per side. Gently remove with tongs or slotted spoon; drain well on paper toweling. Repeat until all dough has been fried.

7. Roll warm doughnut strips in ⅓ cup (80 mL) sugar to coat lightly. Serve immediately.
Makes about 18 doughnut strips

Bolillos CRUSTY OVAL ROLLS

1 package (¼ ounce or 7 g) active dry yeast
1⅓ cups (330 mL) warm water (105 to 115°F or 40 to 46°C)
1 tablespoon (15 mL) honey
1 tablespoon (15 mL) lard or vegetable shortening, melted and cooled
1½ teaspoons (7 mL) salt
3¼ to 4 cups (810 mL to 1 L) bread flour
¼ cup (60 mL) cold water
1 teaspoon (5 mL) cornstarch

1. Sprinkle yeast over the warm water in large mixer bowl; stir to mix. Let stand 5 minutes.

2. Stir honey, lard and salt into yeast mixture; add 2½ cups (625 mL) flour. Mix at low speed; then beat at medium speed until very elastic, about 5 minutes. Gradually stir in as much of the remaining flour needed to make soft dough, ½ to 1 cup (125 to 250 mL).

3. Knead dough on floured surface, adding just as much remaining flour needed to prevent sticking, until dough is smooth and elastic, 15 to 20 minutes. Place the dough in greased bowl; turn dough over to grease top. Let rise, covered, in warm place until doubled, about 1 hour.

4. Punch down dough; knead briefly on floured surface. Let rest 10 minutes. Divide dough into 10 equal pieces; roll each piece into ball on floured surface with palm of hand.

5. Starting at center and working toward opposite ends, roll each ball on floured surface with palms of hands into oval tapered at both ends. Each piece should be about 5½ inches (14 cm) long and 2 inches (5 cm) wide at center. Place, evenly spaced, on 2 greased baking sheets; let rise, loosely covered, until almost doubled, about 25 minutes.

6. Meanwhile, heat oven to 375°F (190°C). Mix cold water and cornstarch in small saucepan. Heat over high heat, stir-

ring constantly, to boiling; boil until thickened and clear, about 2 minutes.

7. Brush risen rolls with warm cornstarch mixture. Slash each roll lengthwise with razor blade or sharp, thin knife to ½ inch (1.3 cm) from each end, cutting about ½ inch (1.3 cm) deep.

8. Bake until rolls are golden brown and sound hollow when tapped, 30 to 35 minutes. Remove from baking sheets; cool on wire racks.
Makes 10 rolls

Crumble-Top Orange Rolls PAN DULCE DE NARANJA

1 cup (250 mL) milk
⅓ cup (80 mL) sugar
¼ cup (60 mL) lard or
  vegetable shortening
2 teaspoons (10 mL) grated
  orange rind
¾ teaspoon (4 mL) salt
2 packages (¼ ounce or 7 g
  each) active dry yeast
¼ cup (60 mL) warm water
  (105 to 115°F or 40 to 46°C)
3 large eggs
5 to 5½ cups (1250 to
  1375 mL) all-purpose flour
Orange Crumble Topping
  (recipe follows)

1. Scald milk in small saucepan over medium heat; remove from heat. Add sugar, lard, orange rind and salt; stir until lard is melted. Let stand at room temperature until lukewarm, about 10 minutes.

2. Sprinkle yeast over the warm water in large mixer bowl; stir to mix. Let stand 5 minutes.

3. Mix milk mixture and eggs into yeast mixture; add 3 cups (750 mL) flour. Mix at low speed; then beat at medium speed until smooth and elastic,

about 5 minutes. Gradually stir in as much of the remaining flour needed to make soft dough, about 1¾ cups (430 mL).

4. Knead dough on floured surface, adding just as much remaining flour needed to prevent sticking, until dough is smooth and elastic, 10 to 15

minutes. Place the dough in greased bowl; turn dough over to grease top. Let rise, covered, in warm place until doubled, 45 to 60 minutes.

5. Meanwhile, prepare Orange Crumble Topping.

6. Punch down dough; knead briefly on lightly floured surface. Divide into 12 equal pieces; roll each piece into ball. Place balls evenly spaced on 2 greased baking sheets.

7. For each roll, press about 1 tablespoon (15 mL) Orange Crumble Topping between hands into 3-inch (8-cm) circle and place on top of dough ball.

8. For snail design, begin at center and make continuous spiral cut in Topping with tip of small knife. For crisscross design, make parallel cuts in Topping about ½ inch (1.3 cm) apart in both directions.

9. Heat oven to 375°F (190°C). Let rolls rise, loosely covered, in warm place until almost doubled, about 30 minutes.

10. Bake until rolls are light brown and sound hollow when tapped, 20 to 25 minutes. Remove from baking sheets; cool on wire racks.
Makes 12 rolls

Orange Crumble Topping

¾ cup (180 mL) all-purpose
  flour
½ cup (125 mL) sugar
¾ teaspoon (4 mL) ground
  cinnamon
½ teaspoon (2 mL) grated
  orange rind
¼ cup (60 mL) butter or
  margarine, cold
1 large egg yolk
1 teaspoon (5 mL) orange
  juice

1. Mix flour, sugar, cinnamon and orange rind in medium bowl. Cut in butter with pastry blender or 2 knives until mixture has texture of coarse crumbs.

2. Beat egg yolk and orange juice in small bowl; add to flour mixture, stirring with fork until evenly blended.

Pecan Torte TORTA DE PACANA

½ cup (125 mL) pecans
1½ ounces (45 g) Mexican chocolate
⅔ cup (160 mL) butter or margarine, at room temperature
⅔ cup (160 mL) powdered sugar, sifted
4 large eggs, separated, at room temperature
1 teaspoon (5 mL) vanilla
½ cup (125 mL) packaged fine dry bread crumbs
⅛ teaspoon (0.5 mL) cream of tartar
Cream Filling (recipe follows)
Powdered sugar
1 tablespoon (15 mL) shaved Mexican chocolate
Pecan halves

1. Heat oven to 350°F (180°C). Grease and flour 8-inch (20-cm) springform pan.

2. Process ½ cup (125 mL) pecans in blender or food processor with on/off turns until very finely ground; do not overprocess or nuts will become oily. Grate 1½ ounces (45 g) chocolate.

3. Beat butter and ⅓ cup (80 mL) powdered sugar in large mixer bowl until light and fluffy. Add egg yolks, 1 at a time, beating well after each addition; beat in vanilla. Stir in bread crumbs, ground pecans and grated chocolate.

4. Combine egg whites and cream of tartar in small mixer bowl; using clean beaters, beat until soft peaks form. Gradually beat in remaining ⅓ cup (80 mL) powdered sugar; beat until stiff and glossy.

5. Stir about ⅓ egg white mixture into butter mixture to lighten it, then fold in remaining egg white mixture. Spread batter evenly in springform pan.

6. Bake until edges begin to pull away from pan and wooden pick inserted in center comes out clean, 35 to 45 minutes. Cool in pan on wire rack 10 minutes. Remove sides of pan; cool completely, 1 to 1½ hours.

7. Prepare Cream Filling.

8. Cut cake horizontally in half; place bottom on serving plate. Spread Filling evenly over bottom layer; cover with top layer. Refrigerate, covered, at least 2 hours or up to 24 hours.

9. Just before serving, place wire rack on top of torte; sieve powdered sugar over torte. Remove rack. Garnish with shaved chocolate and pecan halves.

Makes 6 to 8 servings

Cream Filling

3 ounces (85 g) Mexican chocolate, chopped
1 cup (250 mL) whipping cream
2 teaspoons (10 mL) coffee-flavored liqueur or coffee
1 teaspoon (5 mL) vanilla

1. Combine chocolate and 2 tablespoons (30 mL) cream in top of double boiler; heat over simmering water, stirring occasionally, until smooth. Stir in liqueur; remove from water. Let stand at room temperature to cool slightly, 10 minutes.

2. Combine remaining cream and the vanilla in chilled small mixer bowl; beat until stiff. Fold in chocolate mixture; refrigerate until ready to use.

Makes about 2 cups (500 mL)

Flaming Bananas PLATANOS FLAMEADOS

4 large scoops rich vanilla or coffee ice cream (about 1 pint or 500 mL)
10 ripe finger bananas or 4 regular-size bananas
¼ cup (60 mL) butter or margarine
¼ cup (60 mL) piloncillo
½ cup (125 mL) fresh orange juice
2 tablespoons (30 mL) fresh lime juice
2 tablespoons (30 mL) coffee-flavored liqueur
¼ cup (60 mL) golden rum

1. Place 1 scoop ice cream in each of 4 dessert dishes in freezer.

2. Just before serving, peel bananas; cut lengthwise into halves. (If using regular bananas, cut each half crosswise into thirds.)

3. Melt butter in 10-inch (25-cm) skillet over medium-high heat. Stir in piloncillo; add orange juice and lime juice. Cook, stirring frequently, until sauce is thick and syrupy, 6 to 8 minutes.

4. Add bananas to sauce; cook, turning gently, just to heat through and coat with sauce, about 1 minute. Gently stir in liqueur. Remove from heat.

5. Heat rum in very small saucepan over low heat just until barely warm to touch, about 30 seconds; do not allow to bubble. Pour rum over hot banana mixture; immediately ignite with long match. Stir with long-handled spoon until flames subside.

6. Place warm bananas around ice cream; spoon sauce over top. Serve immediately.

Makes 4 servings

Fruited Rice Pudding ARROZ CON LECHE Y FRUTAS

½ cup (125 mL) golden raisins
½ cup (125 mL) diced dried apricots or candied fruit peel
Hot water
1 small orange
2 cups (500 mL) water
1 cup (250 mL) raw long-grain rice
1½-inch (4-cm) piece cinnamon stick
2 cups (500 mL) milk
⅔ cup (160 mL) sugar
3 large egg yolks
½ cup (125 mL) half & half
½ cup (125 mL) diced pitted dates
¼ cup (60 mL) toasted flaked coconut

1. Combine raisins and apricots in small bowl; add hot water to cover. Let stand at room temperature 15 minutes; drain.

2. Pare rind from ½ the orange in long strips, taking care not to remove white pith along with rind. (Reserve orange for other use.)

3. Heat 2 cups (500 mL) water in large saucepan over medium-high heat to boiling.

Stir in rice, orange rind and cinnamon stick; reduce heat to low. Simmer, covered, until rice is almost tender, about 15 minutes.

4. Scald milk in small saucepan. Stir milk and sugar into rice mixture; simmer over low heat, stirring constantly, until milk is absorbed, about 15 minutes. Remove from heat; remove and discard orange rind and cinnamon stick.

5. Whisk egg yolks and half & half in small bowl. Gradually add about 1 cup (250 mL) hot rice mixture to yolk mixture, mixing well. Gradually add yolk mixture to remaining rice mixture in pan, mixing well.

6. Cook pudding over low heat, stirring constantly, until yolk mixture has been absorbed, about 2 minutes; immediately transfer to bowl. Stir in raisins, apricots and dates; refrigerate, covered, until cold, at least 3 hours. Serve, sprinkled with coconut.

Makes 8 servings

Caramel Custard **FLAN**

1 cup (250 mL) sugar
1 vanilla bean
2 cups (500 mL) half & half
1 cup (250 mL) milk
6 large eggs
2 large egg yolks
Hot water
Fresh whole and sliced
    strawberries

1. Heat oven to 325°F (160°C). Place 5½- to 6-cup (1375-mL to 1.5-L) ring mold in oven until hot, about 10 minutes.

2. Place ½ cup (125 mL) sugar in heavy medium skillet; cook over medium-high heat, stirring frequently, until completely melted and deep amber color, 5 to 8 minutes. Do not allow sugar to burn.

3. Immediately pour caramelized sugar into ring mold; holding mold with potholder, quickly rotate to coat bottom and sides evenly with sugar. Place mold on wire rack. (**Caution**: Caramelized sugar is *very* hot; do not touch it.)

4. Cut vanilla bean lengthwise in half; combine with half & half and milk in heavy 2-quart (2-L) saucepan. Heat over medium heat until almost simmering; remove from heat. Stir in remaining ½ cup (125 mL) sugar until dissolved; remove vanilla bean.*

5. Lightly beat eggs and egg yolks in large bowl until blended but not foamy; gradually stir in milk mixture. Pour custard into ring mold.

6. Place mold in large baking pan; pour hot water into baking pan to depth of ½ inch (1.3 cm). Bake until knife inserted into center of custard comes out clean, 35 to 40 minutes.

7. Remove mold from water bath; place on wire rack. Let stand 30 minutes. Refrigerate, covered, until cold throughout, 1½ to 2 hours.

8. To serve, loosen inner and outer edges of custard with tip of small knife. Cover mold with rimmed serving plate; invert and lift off mold. Garnish with strawberries. Spoon some of the melted caramel over each serving.
    Makes 6 to 8 servings

Vanilla bean can be saved for future use; rinse well, pat dry and place in container of sugar. Use vanilla-flavored sugar to sweeten fruits and baked desserts.

Pecan Shortbread Cookies **POLVORONES**

1 cup (250 mL) sugar
½ cup (125 mL) butter or
    margarine, at room
    temperature
½ cup (125 mL) lard or
    vegetable shortening, at
    room temperature
1 large egg yolk
1 teaspoon (5 mL) vanilla
2¼ cups (560 mL) all-
    purpose flour
¾ teaspoon (4 mL) ground
    cinnamon
¼ teaspoon (1 mL) anise
    seeds, finely crushed
Pinch salt
½ cup (125 mL) finely
    chopped pecans

1. Combine ¾ cup (180 mL) sugar, the butter and lard in large mixer bowl; beat until light and fluffy. Add egg yolk and vanilla; beat until smooth.

2. Mix flour, cinnamon, anise seeds and salt in medium bowl. Add flour mixture, ¼ at a time, to butter mixture, stirring to blend well after each addition. Stir in pecans.

3. Heat oven to 350°F (180°C). Place remaining ¼ cup (60 mL) sugar in small bowl.

4. For each cookie, pinch off piece of dough the size of small walnut (enough to make about 1-inch or 2.5-cm ball). Roll dough between palms into ball; roll ball in sugar to coat. Place balls 3 inches (8 cm) apart on ungreased baking sheets.

5. Press each ball with bottom of glass to flatten into ⅜-inch (1-cm) thick circle, dipping glass into sugar each time to prevent sticking.

6. Bake cookies 10 minutes. Reduce oven setting to 300°F (150°C); continue baking until cookies are light brown, 12 to 15 minutes longer.

7. Let cookies cool slightly on baking sheets set on wire racks, 2 to 3 minutes. Transfer cookies from baking sheets to racks; cool completely.
Makes about 3 dozen cookies

Coconut Empanadas EMPANADAS DE COCO

Orange-Coconut Filling
  (recipe follows)
1½ cups (375 mL) all-
  purpose flour
3½ tablespoons (52 mL)
  sugar
1½ teaspoons (7 mL) baking
  powder
½ teaspoon (2 mL) salt
¼ cup (60 mL) butter or
  margarine, cold
2 tablespoons (30 mL) lard or
  vegetable shortening, cold
2½ to 3½ tablespoons (37 to
  52 mL) cold water
2 tablespoons (30 mL) milk

1. Prepare Orange-Coconut
Filling.

2. Mix flour, 2 tablespoons
(30 mL) sugar, the baking
powder and salt in medium

bowl. Cut in butter and lard
with pastry blender or 2 knives
until mixture forms coarse
crumbs.

3. Sprinkle 1 tablespoon
(15 mL) cold water at a time
over flour mixture, stirring and
tossing lightly with fork, just
until dough clings together.
Shape dough into 1-inch
(2.5-cm) thick circle.

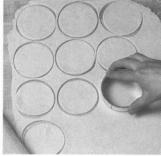

4. Roll out dough on lightly
floured surface to ⅛-inch
(3-mm) thickness. Cut dough
into circles using 3¼-inch
(8.5-cm) round cutter. Gather
trimmings into ball; reroll and
cut out additional circles.

5. Heat oven to 375°F (190°C).
Place 1 teaspoon (5 mL)
Orange-Coconut Filling on
bottom half of each circle, leaving ½-inch (1.3-cm) edge uncovered. Brush edges lightly
with water. Fold top half of
dough over filling; press edges
together with fork to seal.

6. Arrange empanadas 2
inches (5 cm) apart on lightly
greased baking sheet. Brush
tops lightly with milk; sprinkle

lightly with remaining 1½ tablespoons (22 mL) sugar.

7. Bake empanadas until light
brown, 15 to 18 minutes. Remove from baking sheet; cool
on wire rack.
  Makes 14 to 16 empanadas

Orange-Coconut Filling

⅓ cup (80 mL) sugar
1 large egg
1 tablespoon (15 mL) orange
  juice
1½ teaspoons (7 mL) lime
  juice
½ teaspoon (2 mL) grated
  orange rind
Pinch salt
1 tablespoon (15 mL) butter
  or margarine
2 tablespoons (30 mL) flaked
  coconut

1. Combine sugar, egg, orange
juice, lime juice, orange rind
and salt in top of double boiler;
whisk until blended. Add
butter.

2. Cook mixture over simmering water, stirring frequently,
until very thick, 10 to 12 minutes. Stir in coconut; transfer to
small bowl. Refrigerate, covered, until completely cool,
about 30 minutes.

Mexican Chocolate Mousse DULCE DE CHOCOLATE

6 to 6½ ounces (170 to 185 g)
  Mexican chocolate,
  coarsely chopped
1½ cups (375 mL) whipping
  cream
3 tablespoons (45 mL) golden
  rum, if desired
¾ teaspoon (4 mL) vanilla
Sliced almonds

1. Combine chocolate and 3 tablespoons (45 mL) cream in
top of double boiler; heat over
simmering water, stirring occasionally, until smooth. Gradually stir in rum; remove from
water. Let stand at room temperature to cool slightly, 15
minutes.

2. Combine remaining cream
and vanilla in chilled small
mixer bowl; beat until stiff.

3. Gently fold whipped cream
into cooled chocolate mixture
until uniform in color. Spoon
mousse into 4 individual dessert dishes; refrigerate until
firm, 2 to 3 hours. Garnish with
almonds.
  Makes 4 servings

Index